You'll Laugh
About This
Someday

DEVOTIONS
FOR FRAZZLED MOMS

Melissa Howell

 **Pacific Press®**
Publishing Association

Nampa, Idaho | Oshawa, Ontario, Canada
www.pacificpress.com

Cover design by Steve Lanto
Cover design resources from iStockphoto
Inside design by Kristin Hansen-Mellish

The author assumes full responsibility for the accuracy of all facts and quotations as cited in this book.

You can obtain additional copies of this book by calling toll-free 1-800-765-6955 or by visiting http://www.adventistbookcenter.com.

ISBN 978-0-8163-5783-3

September 2015

Dedication

To my mommy,
Terry Elaine Palmer,

who told us every day, in every way,
that motherhood was the greatest joy of her life.

Table of Contents

Acknowledgments

Caleb, Toby, Wyatt and Brooke—Thanks for being my kiddos. I love each of you with all of my heart. I could never explain how much joy you bring to my life. But I can say that sometimes just a smile, a giggle, or a hug is enough to make my heart feel like bursting. One day when you grow up and realize that all of these chapters are about you—please forgive me. Grow up some more, have your own children, and then you will finally know just exactly how much I love you. *And,* how much work, and joy, and beauty, and madness it all is.

Angela Pierce—If I hadn't dedicated this book to my Mom, I would have dedicated it to you (better luck next time, haha). No other mommy has shared the journey of motherhood with me as much as you have. Thanks for being on the other end of all my crazy, hilarious, disgusting, or depressing texts. Thanks for reading all these chapters. Thanks for having an awful memory so my secrets are always safe. Thanks for a hundred adventures on sunny days, and a hundred afternoons of couch-sitting and wall-staring on rainy days. Thanks for providing three beautiful wives for my three sons. Thanks for the casseroles. Thanks for your friendship.

Thanks to my writing group: Melanie Bockmann, Seth Pierce, and Greg Howell. Melanie, editor extraordinaire—thanks for your feedback on every last chapter. I have learned so much about writing from you. It was you who first helped me form the vision for this book. Seth, thanks for reading about a quarter of the chapters I sent you. You have taught me more about humor than anyone else. Thanks for laughing at all my misfortunes, and helping me turn them into stories. Thanks for the daily texts of "get writing, Missy!" You've been a faithful friend. Be saved.

My husband Greg—Thanks for reading every single one of these chapters. Thanks for changing diapers and making sandwiches and doing school pick-up while I wrote. Thanks for never letting me give up on the idea of this book, and for all the sacrifices you made to help me finish it. Thanks for believing in me even when I don't believe in myself. Thanks for being my best friend and companion on this crazy roller coaster of parenting. I don't know how I would do it without you. Thanks for being the best Daddy to our 4 beautiful children, and thanks for being a husband that exceeds even MY expectations. I love you more every single day.

Thanks to my girlfriends and mom-friends who have also shared motherhood with me: Mary Ellen Carlson, Christi Chang, Lizzie Mattson, Lauren Proctor, Kerri Purkeypile, Janella Riter, Katy Paise, Rochelle Everett, Melissa Baskett, Renee Rasco, April Johnson, Peggy Cress (NEET), Andrea Lunde, Alicia Johnston, and Rachel Johnson, whose writing has so often inspired my own. I praise God for putting you ladies in my life. I have learned something important from each one of you. Thanks for your examples of what it means to be a Christian mom in the real world. Thanks for your messy houses too—I especially appreciate that!

Thanks to my sisters and cousins: Heather Colburn, Brittny Palmer, Sarah Palmer, Carin Howell, Angel Shockey, Avri Colburn, and Miki-Mon—I'm so blessed to have a family full of strong, spirit-filled, amazing women!

I am grateful for all the other women in my family who have given me incredible examples of strength, wisdom, patience and dedication: Shirley, Noni, Schleria, Gwen, Sheryal, Rose, Gayle, Linda, Wanda, and Ros.

Bill Roberts—Thanks for being a spiritual mentor, and for being a pastor to the pastors. You have faithfully seen us through so many struggles. Thanks for sharing the journey.

Ivan and Ila Zbaraschuk—I never would have made it through those first few months of infant twins without your food and friendship. Thank you.

Thanks to my writing chair by the forest window: you supported me every minute. Thanks for giving me perspective, and for always letting me lean on you.

Washington—Thank you for Rosario Beach, Little Mountain Park, Kalaloch, Lake Crescent, Mount Rainier, Excelsior Pass, the Skagit Valley tulip fields, Friday Harbor, and the dozens of other beaches and trails and coastlines that have filled my soul with wonder and my car with sand and rocks.

Lastly, thank you to my own Mommy and Daddy, who gave me the best childhood on earth. There's never been any doubt in my mind that I am loved. Thanks for rope swings and slumber parties and family vacations, and for *always* having time to listen. Thank you for a hundred memories, a thousand sacrifices, and the one thing that matters most: a relationship with Jesus. I can only hope to be half the parent that each of you are.

Marathon

Getting hit in the eyeball with a whipping rope was what finally sent me over the edge.

It had been one of those days . . .

I awoke to the sound of *both* babies crying and came in to find them both soaked to the skin in their own pee. My husband and I had a stupid argument before he left. One twin ate a handful of dirt from my gardenia plant while I cooked breakfast. The other wouldn't stop crying unless I held her, so I cooked with one hand (I've really become quite good at this). We left the next day's fireworks out on the table for some awful reason, and my six-year-old asked approximately forty-five times during breakfast if we could go outside *right now*, RIGHT NOW and light off this one, or that one, or how about this . . . (specific one). I yelled at the neighbor kid whose face was shamelessly smashed against our front window for ten minutes—only to discover that his mom had heard me from the driveway. She-twin spit cereal onto my new purple silk robe that I had saved a month for and worn for the first time that day. He-twin stealth-pooped all the way up his back, and of course I didn't discover it until it rubbed against—you guessed it—the purple silk robe.

Finally, I had gotten the poop cleaned up and breakfast put away to a point where I could feed the second baby. The six-year-old had decided to play cowboys, singing the same one line of the worst song on earth over and over and over. From somewhere upstairs, I could hear the three-year-old yelling, "Come wipe my bottom! Mommy! Come wipe my bottom!" The first baby clawed my leg for attention while the second refused to open her locked jaw, and the six-year-old asked whether we could light just one firework, *again*, and—right at that moment—*pow!* The end of the cowboy's rope slashed me directly in the eyeball. Burning. Blazing. Stinging.

And I Lost. My. Mind.

First I screamed. Lots of angry words. Loudly. Which made the babies both immediately start sobbing. Then I grabbed the prized rope and threw it in the trash: cue the six-year-old to begin wailing. The three-year-old saddling the toilet was now crying from upstairs, and I figured since everyone else was crying, well, heck—I might as well join them.

We all cried together for what seemed like quite a while, my children and I. They were scared and sad and wounded by my outburst, but me—I was defeated. I began to spiral down into that dark dungeon of mommyhood where you wonder why you ever had kids to begin with, how you can possibly face another minute of this misery, and what would happen if you just stood up and walked out the door and never came back. (I am told all mommies have these thoughts from time to time. But that doesn't make it any better.)

Parenting young children has often been compared to running a marathon, and rightly so—a marathon is about training, pacing, fitness, endurance, determination, pain, suffering, misery, and victory. My communications teacher in college, Chris Blake, once told a story about a marathon he saw on TV that I think of often as a parent. Long after all the other runners had crossed the finish line, the TV cameras were following one unfortunately large woman who was about two full hours behind the crowd. And it was no wonder why—she wasn't running, she was all but hobbling, with the poise of a walrus on land. It took monumental energy just to lift one foot at a time. A paper cup casually blowing past on the street was making faster progress than she was. Not only would she certainly be the last to finish, but it was doubtful whether she would ever finish at all, at the rate she was going. This was the "fat lady," and singing the final song would have to be upstaged by simple breathing.

But Mr. Blake noticed something that riveted him to this poor plodder. With each leaden step the woman took, she was muttering something to herself. After a minute, he realized that she was saying the exact same thing every time she smacked the pavement. Fascinated, he kept watching in hopes that the cameras would zoom in close enough to read her lips and clarify the phrase.

They did.

Every time the woman lifted her right leg, she pointedly mouthed, "Oh God." And every time she lifted her left, she finished, "I can."

Oh God, I can.

Oh God, I can.

Oh God. I *can.*

All the way to the finish line.

In the marathon of motherhood, this mantra really works for me. When the daily grind is grinding me just a little too fine, I try to take a second, catch my breath, and whisper, "Oh God, I can." When each and every leaden step of the day anchors me in discouragement and self-doubt, I remind myself, "Oh God, I can." When loneliness and exhaustion stalk me like shadows, a simple "Oh God, I can" is enough to take another step. Sometimes it's a pep talk. Other days it's a plea for help. And often

I don't even believe it initially, but the repetition has a way of rooting itself.

Later, during a quiet moment (just kidding, I don't have any of those—actually it was while I was showering to what I call the argument soundtrack), I was reflecting on the rope incident and the marathon woman, and I somehow thought of Jesus. Jesus in Gethsemane. Mud under His fingernails, clawing the ground in abject anguish. "Oh God, I can't!" He faints. Blood speckles the dust. An angel is sent to renew His strength. "Oh God, I can," He whispers. And then, "Oh God, I *will*." The beam's crushing weight, the nails' piercing agony—"Oh God, I can." Calvary was His finish line, and He crossed it for me.

That marathon woman crossed the finish line too, believe it or not. Four hours after everyone else, but—she finished. And as she finally stepped over that blessed line she was still repeating, now cheering victoriously, "Oh God—I can!"

My finish line that day was bedtime, but since it was a long time until that holy hour, there were a lot of other things I realized I *could* do: I apologized to my children for losing my temper. I sent an apology note to the mother of the annoying kid I yelled at. The prized rope came out of the trash. One firework was selected and lit off. And for myself, I took a nap on the floor while one baby beat me over the head with a stuffed animal the entire time. Yes. I really did sleep.

My other finish line (besides college) is heaven. Since I'm hoping my children will cross it with me, I'm training today with them in mind. Give up a priceless hour of sleep to pray (beg) for patience and wisdom? Oh God, I can. Wrap my arms around a child I'd just as soon strangle? Oh God, I can. Model forgiveness when it's hard, endure a day of tasks I hate, make time for moments of wonder? Oh God, I can. Lavish grace as often as possible, just as grace has been lavished on me?

Oh God—with Your help—I can.

(Maybe there will be a purple silk robe waiting for me beyond the pearly gates?)

IN CASE YOU GET SIX MINUTES TO YOURSELF: STUDY GUIDE

1. What is your particular race right now—in motherhood, marriage, and life?
2. How are you running your race: at a sprint, a steady pace, a limp, or a crawl?
3. What things threaten your long-term endurance? What things strengthen it?
4. Read the chapter "Gethsemane" (chapter 74) in the book *The Desire of Ages* by Ellen White, specifically pages 690–693. What was the turning point in Jesus' marathon of grief that night? When was the exact moment and what was the exact reason that Jesus ultimately decided to go through the horrors of Calvary?
5. Read Hebrews 12:1–3, where Paul talks about running the race of the Christian life with endurance. What is the secret?
6. Where does the "Oh God, I can" belong in your life today?

The Snail

Please, Mommy! Please! Please can we buy a pet snail too! *PLEEEEEEEZE?"*

We are at the pet store on a September afternoon. We came here to replace the fish that died in the boys' fish tank the night before. "One fish, and one fish only!" I had warned my boys all the way here. In my hands are two bags. Each has a fish swimming skittishly inside. And now they are begging me for a third animal—a snail. I am teetering on the edge of angry.

It's not the worst thing, I try to tell myself, as I hear the birds squawking from ten aisles away. *A water snail is a nice quiet pet—but wait, No! I specifically told them:* One. Fish. The inner Mommy dialogue with myself begins: *Do they think they can take advantage of my generosity? Do they have no respect for my clear and firm boundaries? When is it going to be time for Mommy to show that her limitations mean business around here? Today! No snail.*

The "helpful" pet shop employee is staring at me. She has already spent fifteen minutes fishing out two very specific "That one! That one!" fish for me. I suddenly realize she's waiting for my response now—snail or no snail? I have won the argument in my head, but it appears I haven't answered my children in real life yet. *Getting to that, net-wielding lady, getting to that. She's going to judge me if I say No to a harmless three-dollar snail, isn't she? Oh, I am* not *in any mood to be judged today!*

"There is something you should know about snails," she breaks into my self-talk. "They need algae to live on. So, I mean, if you get a snail? You like, have to make sure you never clean the tank. Ever. Just let that algae grow and grow so the snail can eat it and stuff."

See, now she's done it! I will never be able to say No to my children with an explanation like . . . wait. Wait. *Did she just say I can stop cleaning the tank? Does that mean— forever? No more Olympic balancing moves with watery endings, no more sifting fish poop thick as volcano silt, no more tank rocks on my driveway for months? No cleaning the tank! Hallelujah!*

"I will take two snails!" I exclaim with sudden glee.

"Yaaaayyyy!" my kids burst into celebration. "We are getting a snail! Two snails! Yay yay yay yay! You are the best Mommy *ever*! *Snaaaa-ails! Snaaa-ails! Snaaaa-ails!*" They chant and hand-wave and hop-dance around the fish tank area. I am tempted to take their hands and dance with them, I'm so relieved. The clever employee hurriedly fishes out any two snails she pleases, before the victors think to attach to a very specific certain pair.

In a few minutes we are checking out at the registers with our *two* fish and our *two* get-out-of-tank-cleaning-jail-free snails. My boys bounce out to the car, and I carefully cradle the large bag containing our new family members. I am already planning to name one delightful snail Pac-Man and the other Roomba. My kids will understand someday, I figure.

"Tank cleaners!" I congratulate myself. "What a great day this has turned out to be. Leave the filth—the snails will clean it."

But driving home it hit me: the similarity. I think I am the snail of my own household.

Everybody else seems to make messes at will and knowingly leave them all for me to clean up faithfully, as if that's my sole purpose in life. As if that's exactly what I was made to accomplish. They keep scattering toys and throwing food on the floor and dirtying clothes and soiling their own bottoms as if it's their personal job to make sure I still have work to do. "Don't clean anything up," I imagine them thinking, "or Mom won't have any reason for existing!" So they cover entire windows in handprints. They smear toothpaste across the counters. They pull every last book from the giant bookcase. To make sure that the snail still has duty and purpose in life.

I don't like being the snail.

At times I have even begun to resent being the snail. Quite bitterly. I fume about being trapped in an endless exhausting cycle of running the dishwasher and emptying the drier and changing diapers two at a time and sweeping the floor that can never stay clean for longer than three minutes. And there is no way out of this cycle—I have to keep doing it, and doing it, and doing it—all day. Every day. For years and years into the future. Nobody can rescue me from it and I can't stop, because to ignore the cleaning would make things even more miserable than cleaning is. The other day as I was sweeping the kitchen floor, I thought to myself, *I will still be sweeping this floor on the day my kids leave for college. I will never be done sweeping this floor.*

I wish someone had told me during my own college years that so much of my day would be spent doing so many menial tasks. I foolishly thought my life would be all about the ideas and concepts I was learning and loving more each semester. "Oh no, girlfriend," I wish they had said. "You may think about those far-off ideas from time to time—but your life? Honey. It's gonna be about scrubbing toilets and showers. You're going to spend hours each day trying to feed a small crowd three times, and clean up after each time. You're going to pick up the same exact toys 35,732 times.

A month. You will change more urine-soaked sheets than you could ever count. And you will lose yourself in this—it will threaten to become your identity: the cleaner. The snail."

The truth is—I do lose myself. Often. The lists of things to clean and fix and put away can get so long that I forget there's more to my life. Sometimes I manage to remember things I used to love, dreams I used to have. But there just is no time for those things today. Or tomorrow. Maintaining takes everything I've got. It feels like one of the deepest challenges of motherhood—just fighting to remember who you were and what you wanted before you had kids.

It's after bedtime now, and I have come sneaking back into my sleeping boys' room to watch the little snails, happily scooting around the tank, leaving clean slug-print tracks through the green mosaic of algae. They never stop cleaning, I realize. They will clean all day and night. "How are you happy doing this all day and night, little snails?" I want to ask them. And why aren't I?

Mostly because I'm not actually a snail, I guess. I was made for more than cleaning all day. It isn't my calling or my identity, even if it is my constant activity. My identity is so, *so* much richer. How long has it been since I've considered the things God says about me?

One of the clearest pronouncements Jesus makes about human identity and calling is found in Matthew 5. If I try to imagine the scene, I can see Jesus looking out at the multitudes sitting cross-legged on the grassy hillsides of Galilee. With pride dancing in His eyes, He announces, "You are the light of the world" (verse 14). Having just previously been compared to salt, I assume some people's brows furrow, minds race ahead to guess what He means this time. Chins lift stiffly off palms, heads tilt inquisitively, eyes squint through the afternoon sun as Jesus goes on to explain that a city on a hill cannot be hidden. Perhaps they think of a city they've once seen, or look across the countryside at familiar buildings perched atop a nearby hill. "People don't light a lamp just to put it under a bowl either," Jesus continues (verse 15, author's translation). Giggles escape the mouths of children who picture this silly idea, whispering to their mothers, "Why would anybody do that, Mommy?"

"I don't know, sweetie," she answers, "but *shhh*! I want to listen!" And then Jesus delivers the punch line the crowds were waiting for: "In the same way, let your light shine before others, that they may see your good deeds and glorify your Father in heaven" (verse 16). A pause. A silence settles in as men scratch their beards and women stroke the soft hair of their children, digesting this new idea. Realizing that Jesus has just placed a calling upon their lives.

He's placed that calling on me as well, and on every mother who's in danger of losing sight of her purpose. We are the light of the world too. Maybe not in much of the world, but most definitely within the little worlds of our homes. I am that city on the hill that my children can see from any angle of any room. And it doesn't matter what else I am occupied with all day long—*this* is my real job. To make sure my light is shining, free of baskets. To make sure the lamps of my faith are lit brightly enough that my children will come to recognize the familiar glow of belief. So that maybe one day if their own paths should become very dark, they will search the night for that hill-city's flickering lights, remembering the faith they first learned at my feet, and use its beacon to guide themselves home. This is my real calling, and this is no small calling.

When my husband and I hiked the Grand Canyon several years ago, we took no notice of the South Rim Village shops and windows as we descended the Bright Angel trail by daylight. But once the sun sank and the canyon fell into blackness, we noticed the village lights immediately, flickering above us on the edge of the rim. We could see those lights from almost anywhere in the camp that night, glowing in the dark, marking where we had come from. That's exactly what I am called to give my children: an internal compass of light they can see and access from anywhere. They might not notice it now. One day, however, should they plunge into blackness while desperately scanning the horizon for a light, they will remember where they came from.

How can I be sure that I'm fulfilling this solemn duty, this giant task? One thing I know for certain is that I cannot get lost in being the snail. I can't let the chores list summarize who I am. I have to make sure that God is the One telling me who I am, consistently, all day long—or at least half as often as I pick up a broom or a spatula or a dish towel. In order for Him to be able to do that, I have to create avenues in my life in which His Word can shape me. I need His voice to repeatedly remind me what my greater purpose in this house really is: that I am the light of my kids' world.

Even though I may have to spend a considerable amount of time cleaning my children's hands and faces and bottoms, I'm called to also pass on the kind of values to them that will inspire them to live clean lives. To pass on beauty and wonder, self-control, patience, gratitude, and faith. I am not merely to make clean tracks through the mayonnaise on the kitchen floor (true story), but to make tracks of faithfulness and belief through hard times. I am not in charge of cleaning up their hearts or their souls, but I am solemnly commissioned to introduce them to the only One who can. When they see my light, Jesus says it will lead them to glorify their Father in heaven. And that is, ultimately, what I want for my children the most. Alongside all the cleaning, I must make deliberate efforts to keep sight of this goal.

But in the midst of all this snail-esque cleaning and lamp-shining business, I get the added bonus of enjoying my children, every moment I allow myself to. I get to love them—oh so much—until my heart could almost burst. I get to spend carefree afternoons at pet stores basking in the joy of being the "greatest Mommy on earth" because I bought two simple snails. I get to stand here in the night and watch them sleeping, peaceful and perfect. There won't always be blueberries to clean off my walls, legos stealthily filling my rain boots, or nerf gun bullets waiting under my pillow at night. I won't always be sopping up puddles on my bathroom floor from where my twins happily fished elbows-deep in the toilet. All these bizarre chores together herald one very sacred truth: I have children of my own to treasure. There are so many who would do all the cleaning in the world in order to be able to say the same.

OK. It's worth it. I guess all the cleaning is worth it, in the end.

Clean on, little snails, into the night. Clean on faithfully, as will I.

IN CASE YOU GET SIX MINUTES TO YOURSELF: STUDY GUIDE

1. If you got to choose one household chore that you never had to do again, which one would it be?
2. What cycles of motherhood do you feel yourself getting stuck in?
3. Which duties of motherhood do you feel are most important? Which ones do you take the most joy in?
4. Read Matthew 5:13–16. What are some tangible, practical ways you can be "salt" and "light" to your children?
5. How can you make sure your identity as a person does not get lost during these hectic years of young motherhood?
6. How does one firmly root their identity in God instead of production?
7. Which areas of your own life could use a good cleaning right now?

Houseplants

Y ou can usually tell the state of my soul by coming into my home and observing the state of my houseplants. If they are dry, withered, or drooping, or they appear sapped of all life, you can believe I myself am feeling the exact same way. The plants are frighteningly indicative of my own deficiencies. Their silent witness gives me away: it's been a long hard week (or month), I haven't had a minute to myself, my courage is drooping, and my weary heart is thirsty just like they are. The same goes for when they are alert, well fed, and full of life—I've been well fed lately also. I've taken time to put my life, and my house, in order.

Once I read a quote that said, "A Bible that is falling apart usually belongs to someone who isn't." I liked it so much that I scribbled it into the cover of my own personal Bible—a kind of voluntary self-trial, in a way, leaving myself open for anyone who may find it lying around to ask, Is it well loved, well used? I admit that spending all day in a house with four young children does not provide the best opportunities for Bible study. Getting up early after nursing six to eight times through the night or staying up late with frayed nerves and drooping eyes doesn't help much either. No wonder my houseplants, and my Bible, are neglected: so am I.

About a year ago on a trip to Arizona to see my eighty-nine-year-old grandmother, I came upon her own personal Bible that she has used over the decades—since she became an Adventist in her early twenties. Her Bible, truly, is falling apart—sections can be removed, the leather cover is cracked, peeling, torn, and completely missing in places. The pages are worn, marked, dog-eared, and underlined as if her life depended on it (maybe it did).

Instantly upon seeing this Bible, I wanted it. What a testimony to my grandmother's life—a woman who clings to Jesus, talks of Jesus, and knows Jesus better than most anyone I know. Since she has taken to dedicating items to this or that one of her thirty-plus grandchildren lately, I anxiously flipped open the front cover to see whether there was a dedication written on the first page. My heart sank as I read this inscription: "To be given to Russell Leon Palmer III [my little brother] in the event of my death." I was more disappointed than you might find it reasonable to believe. How I wanted that Bible, intended for my little brother, who may or may not even care a lick about it! How special it would be to *me*! There was nothing else of hers I could ever have wanted more.

Grandma was standing nearby in her bathrobe and slippers, slowly getting ready for bed. I was afraid of revealing just how much I wanted the Bible, because it was likely I'd get rejected or turned down for my brother, who is the namesake of her dear husband. But every time I'm with my grandma, I am also painfully aware that I don't know for certain when I'll see her again. If there's something I need to say, I've learned to say it right then. And so, tentatively, as she rubbed her face cream into her cheeks, I began to express how very much it would mean to me to have the Bible she read every day, after she was gone. "I have to have it!" I pleaded quietly. "It would just mean the world to me."

She didn't say much. She kept getting ready for bed—she tires so easily now, and I could tell she was extremely tired that night. It was clear she wasn't interested in signing away her belongings just then. I hoped that maybe someday later, she would remember my request and change the inscription. I said good night.

What Grandma ended up actually doing was even more than I could have ever hoped for. Several months later, when I was back home in Washington, my parents came to visit us. As is her custom within minutes of arriving at my house, my mother began to unpack countless clothes, toys, trinkets, and treats she had brought for my kids. I only paid half-attention while this classic showering of gifts took place, until all of a sudden there was my grandma's Bible, in her hands, and she was holding it out to me. "Here—this is for you," she said. "Grandma said you told her you had to have it, and so she wanted me to bring it to you right away."

I was speechless. Quite a few thoughts went through my head all together: *She's still alive—isn't she still reading it? Why did she give it to me now?* And then, *It's mine! She heard me. She remembered.*

I now have the Bible sitting on my nightstand beside my bed. It is an unspeakable treasure to me—if there were ever a fire in my home, it's one of the few things I would grab to take out with me. It is also a constant inspiration to me. I look at its broken, faded cover most days of my life, and I usually think, *How unlike my houseplants. They reflect the care I've been giving or denying myself. But this Book, the more disheveled it looks, it testifies of a soul well fed and cared for.*

Society and the media today will tell you all sorts of ways to take care of yourself: eat healthy, buy this product, try this diet, enjoy this guilty pleasure, take this vacation, etc. We all know the basics of what self-care looks like: we need to get enough sleep, enough sun, enough fruits and veggies, (have an excuse why we don't) get some exercise, and make some time for ourselves. Even Grandma used to give me pointers: floss, use a leave-in conditioner, paint your nails every Friday afternoon for Sabbath, and find a hobby you love.

Might I suggest another route of self-care, though? One you might not hear the media touting? Here it is: Open your Bible. Read it daily. Mine it deep for the deficiencies that stare you in the face every day: not enough patience, parched for wisdom, hungry for meaning. Run to its shelter when you're discouraged, desperate, or dead-dog tired. Bask in its encouragement, fill your thirsty soul with the teachings of a Friend who once called Himself the Water of Life. Dog-ear the pages. Underline verses that speak to you as if your life depends on it (maybe it does). Care for your soul by spending time with its Designer.

And while you're at it with all this great spiritual self-care for your soul . . . why don't you go ahead and water your houseplants too.

IN CASE YOU GET SIX MINUTES TO YOURSELF: STUDY GUIDE

1. What things in your household get neglected when you become busy or stressed?
2. When life moves at a crazy pace, are you more likely to neglect your children, your husband, your friends, or yourself?
3. In what areas are you wilting? In what areas are you well fed?
4. Read Mark 1:35 and some of the surrounding stories before and after. What can you learn from this?
5. What are the biggest obstacles in the way of you spending time in prayer and Bible reading? What strategies have worked for you in the past?
6. Read Psalm 119:105. If you made more time to spend in the Scriptures, what might be the result?
7. What is it that you are truly thirsting for from the Lord today?

Restaurant

I t all started because I wanted those carefree days back.

Before we had children, my husband and I used to spend long, lazy days exploring downtown Seattle. We strolled arm in arm through Pike Place market, stopping to investigate any stand or store that caught our attention. We wandered through back alleys, browsed bookstores for hours, and sampled at least one new deli or restaurant on every trip. The need to keep track of time did not exist. We roamed as we pleased, with no schedules in sight. I don't need to tell you how much I crave these times now, because you already know. Some days it's almost painful to pass a bookstore or a favorite restaurant, but I know the chaos that takes place inside isn't worth it, so I usually just walk on by.

Until I remembered Marrakesh.

On a recent trip through downtown, as we passed by the Moroccan restaurant we once enjoyed, the temptation to revisit those days became too great. Marrakesh might have been our favorite restaurant back then because of its authentic and unique charm. Guests sit on pillows on the ground around short mosaic-inlaid tables and eat other-worldly food under Bedouin-style tent draping and colored glass lamps. Waiters bring bread balanced in large hip baskets and drip orange-blossom water into customers' cupped hands between courses to freshen them. I could almost taste the rose-mango juice, and the thought of smoky lentil soup or buttery couscous over vegetables was more than I could bear.

"Let's stop!" I begged my husband. "It sounds *sooooo* good!"

At first he said nothing, simply raised his eyebrows. Then he looked confused. "Wait—*that* restaurant? With four kids? With infant twins? Hon, it's quiet in there! The kids will yell, and the babies will cry the whole time, and we'll ruin the meal for everyone in the whole place. What are you thinking?"

"I'm thinking I want to eat there," I said firmly. "It's been years, and we love that place. I'm tired of not doing the things we love just because we have kids. I'm sick of them limiting us. Aren't you?"

"Yeah, I am actually," he admitted slowly. "Dinner out would be really nice. It would be wonderful to feel like normal people again, but—"

"Wouldn't it!" I exclaimed. "Oh let's just pretend for a night—pretend we're young and childless for a night, go to a nice restaurant and a bookstore and just relish the things we used to love! I miss it so much sometimes I could just *burst*!"

He thought this over. "That actually sounds fantastic."

"The kids will adapt!" I added with confidence. "The kids can learn. It will be fine, and they will love it."

"And if they don't?" he asked.

"Let's just try it," I suggested. "If it's awful, we can leave."

"OK," he relented, "let's do it. I could really use a night like this. But I'm afraid it might be a mistake."

He was right, of course.

The meal was an absolute disaster. One or the other of the twins cried the entire time, both older boys poured soup into their laps, and one fell backwards off his pillow into the table nearby. Two drinks were toppled. The baby nursing under a cover between me and the table kept me unable to reach my food for most of the meal. The boys didn't like the apricot chicken or the spicy eggplant salad. They refused to eat the flaky philo pastries for dessert because "they are made of paper, Mommy, and we *don't* eat paper!" I could see my husband growing increasingly frustrated and annoyed. Then she-twin was screaming so loudly while I nursed he-twin that older brother Caleb decided to pick her up to comfort her—a perfectly sweet and helpful idea until she lurched backwards in his arms and banged her head on the table with a resounding *GO-O-O-O-ONG!* The shrieks that followed made everyone in the room stop and stare (and judge, most likely). But that wasn't even the lowest point of the meal.

That took place when the belly-dancers emerged from behind the curtains. (Was this new? Or had I completely forgotten about them?) While they shimmied and shook clanging finger cymbals, men began slipping dollar bills into the strappy bands of their decorated skirts. For reasons unknown to me, my three-year-old son decided he must join this beneficiary event. Before I even knew what was happening, my precious little boy was joyfully running up front and slipping money into a dancer's clothing. The two thoughts that simultaneously came into my head were, (1) What kind of habits will this set him up for later in life? and (2) Wait—*where* did he get that dollar bill?

We left Marrakesh with two babies still crying, two boys allegedly still "starving," sixty-five dollars poorer (plus a skirt-donation dollar bill), and our resolve waning. But it wasn't time to give up yet—we wanted this night, we *needed* this night. Stupidly, we determined that our next stop—Elliot Bay Books—would be a much better place for kids.

Wrong.

A bookstore is even quieter than a restaurant, as it turns out (desperate people tend to forget things like this). And hungry, wired, tired children with goose eggs on their heads don't like to be quiet in bookstores at the end of the night. They like to scream louder, in fact. They like to make towers of books to topple over and play tag down the aisles like an elephant stampede. I joined this jungle parade as I chased after them, double-stroller in tow, hissing, "Be quiet! Stop running this *instant*!" When I finally found my mortified husband hiding in the history section, pretending not to know us, the only three words I could muster were, "Let's. Go. *Now.*"

"Are you buying that?" he pointed to a book balancing on the stroller. A parenting book, ironically. I should have bought it, because at that moment, Lord knows, I needed it.

I collected the circus and left the bookstore in defeat. Anger grew in me as we pulled and pushed crying kids through the happy college crowds on the sidewalks. I looked at the people passing: smiling, laughing, joyful people all headed out into the night for a fantastic evening. How I envied them!

I know it sounds ungrateful, but in moments like this it's so easy to start resenting my kids and my life, so easy to feel trapped. I fumed and mourned over all the luxuries we had lost when we had children. I longed for the days of ease gone by. I pouted over my current limitations, questioned for the hundredth time why people even have children at all. And then, we passed him.

He sat slumped in a wheelchair pushed up a few feet away from a flickering television. Through the window of his small, spartan, street-level apartment, I could see his once-handsome face hanging in wrinkles. Quivering hands clutched a remote control, trying hard to change the channel. The apartment was empty and dark, and he filled it alone. He looked at least a hundred years old, weather-worn and life-worn, and distinctly sad. A certain loneliness seemed etched into the ancient lines of his tired face, wrapping him and the little studio in isolation.

"Why are you staring, Mommy?" A tiny voice brought me back to reality, a tiny form tugging my arm. "I'm cold! Let's go home!" I looked down. What I saw holding my hand wasn't just my little boy, it was *life*—life itself. I picked him up then, and hugged him tight, while bookstores and restaurants and all the frustrations of the night submerged under a sea of gratitude. I realized with full force that one day far from now, if I find myself sitting solo in an empty apartment at my life's end, I will look back on nights like this not with anger but with deep joy. Then I will know what it *really* means to crave a life gone by. "Oh God," I pleaded silently in that drizzly Seattle night air, "I don't want to waste this! Please, please help me to be present. Help me to be here, now, instead of wishing I were somewhere else, because these really are some of the best days I will ever know."

The composer of Psalm 90 wrote, "Teach us to number our days, that we may gain a heart of wisdom" (verse 12). The same verse in the New Living Translation reads, "Teach us to make the most of our time," or "Teach us to realize the brevity of life." As a mother of very young children, I need this lesson in numbering and brevity. I often get lost in the disappointments and the details, certain that the diaper days will never end. Captured in a broken clock, I am a passenger waiting on a train platform for a line long gone. But while I'm waiting for my life to start, or come back, in actuality my life is passing.

Something very profound exists in the practice of contemplating our numbered days, or our mortality. When we think about how many or few our days may be, when we see the old man up ahead in the window, the Bible says wisdom results. And by wisdom, I think in this case it means *perspective:* the ability to see what matters and what doesn't. The ancient Hebrew concept of "wisdom" included shrewdness, which is the ability to be a good manager of one's resources. Time is, of course, one of the most valuable resources we possess. So we develop wisdom to manage our time well when we allow a limitless God to teach us that our days are limited.

A few days after the Moroccan restaurant debacle, my mom called to ask how my weekend turned out. I relayed the frustrating night of events to her, mixed with our longings to live like normal people again. She laughed and listened. Then she replied, "Melissa, I am going to tell you a story you have never heard before," which is phenomenal in itself, if you know my mother and her love for repeat story-telling. "A new story?" I swooned sarcastically. "I'm all ears!"

"I remember a day I took you to Sunland Park on a spring afternoon. You were two years old, and I was eight months pregnant with your sister." I can see her young face in my mind's eye, arms stretching over a bursting belly to push me on the swings, back aching and sweat glistening at her temples where it always does when she's working hard. "I felt so exhausted," she admitted, "because it took all my energy to entertain you, and yet you still wanted more, and then another baby was on the way besides. I didn't know where I'd find the time in the day to give both of you the attention you would need." I am tracking with this story so completely. Riveted, in fact. My mother, who always made motherhood look like such an easy joy, suddenly confiding how overwhelmed she felt.

She continued. "I was about to tell you that I couldn't possibly push you anymore, when some older ladies came filing out of the community center behind us. From the paintings and papers they carried, I could tell they had attended an art class. They looked so happy holding their projects, so free, and inside I felt angry at them." Her jealousy was palpable, the same echoes resounding in my very own heart. "So as they passed me at the swing set, carefree and smiling, something inside me couldn't stand being silent. 'I sure wish I had time to take an art class,' I groaned, 'but I would *never* have time for something like that.' One of the ladies stopped beside me," Mom continued, "smiled a sad smile, and said simply this: 'Oh, honey. Cherish *this*! Someday, I promise you, you will have *nothing* but time.' "

And there it was again: the old man in the window, the sand sifting steadily through the hourglass. "It's funny," she added, "because here I am, right where she said I'd be: I have nothing but time. I go out with friends. I wander bookstores. I plant my garden and take long walks. I never would have expected it all to go so fast. But I feel like my most important work is over. Raising you kids—that was the most important thing I ever did."

I'm not sure if she noticed the quiver in my voice when I whispered, "Thank you, Mommy. Thanks for that story." I felt compelled to add, "I don't know if your work is over or not, but I do know that you did an amazing, remarkable job."

"And you are doing an amazing, remarkable job too, sweetie," she insisted. "Hang in there. This time is shorter than anyone could ever explain."

Teach us to number our days.

That image of Mom pushing toddler-me on the swing stays with me, keeps step alongside me on busy days when I start to feel like I'll never live a normal life again. I think of her at home now, clipping daffodils to arrange on a cleared, empty table, and against all odds I actually feel thankful for the dried spaghetti noodles and Transformer setups on mine. I don't know how many days God will allow me on this earth. But I do know that there is a limited time in which my children will live within these messy, noisy rooms. They consume my energy and time today, but in the world of tomorrow I will be running after them for a bit of time. I want to enjoy them while they are here. They aren't stealing something from me, they are giving something to me: the priceless gift of sharing their little lives, the monumental privilege of being their mommy.

Teach us to number our days, O Lord, so that our hearts may learn the wisdom of being thankful for what we have here, and now, while it's ours.

IN CASE YOU GET SIX MINUTES TO YOURSELF: STUDY GUIDE

1. Have you ever experienced an evening like the one described above?
2. When was the last time you felt trapped or resentful in motherhood? What did you do about it?
3. Many women look back on motherhood as the best years of their lives. But while we are living through these years, do we always feel that way? Why or why not?
4. Read Psalm 90:12. What benefits could the suggestion to "number our days" add to motherhood? What stresses might it add?
5. Read the whole chapter of Psalm 90. What place does this verse have in the psalm's greater context? Does this change its meaning any?
6. Read James 1:5–7. What is another way to obtain wisdom, and what are the qualifications of this gift God offers us?
7. In which areas of your life do you most need wisdom today?

Anchors

Sometimes it feels like it would be easier to drag a big metal chain around than to drag my four kids everywhere with me. Take a very simple idea such as going to the store to get milk, for example, and add four kids ages five and under into the picture. What should be an easy little trip turns into a monstrous ordeal and plays out something like this: dress four kids, find eight shoes, put eight shoes on eight feet, find four coats, put four coats on kids, carry kids out to the car, fasten four seatbelts, drive to the store, unfasten four seatbelts, load four kids into a shopping cart, fasten cart belts, shop for the milk, pay for the milk, push the cart to the car, unload the cart, unload four kids back into the car, fasten four seatbelts, realize one shoe is missing, unfasten four seatbelts, load four kids back into the shopping cart, fasten cart belts, troll around the store looking for the lost shoe, abandon the search in desperation, return to the car, unload four kids from the cart into the car, fasten four seat belts, drive home, unfasten four seatbelts, carry each kid into the house, collapse in a chair, accidentally leave the milk to spoil in the car . . .

When just a trip to the grocery store is this ridiculous, you can imagine what a fiasco big events might become, such as going out to eat at restaurants, evenings out, vacations, and holidays. Sometimes it doesn't even feel worth it to leave the house at all. My children hang heavy as anchors, tying me down, mooring me to home, or dragging along in everything I attempt. I've had moments when I wish I could just fling the anchors off and set sail—if only for a day, an hour.

But then, the tides turn.

From the depths of postpartum depression, I suddenly see my little anchors in a drastically different light. On those days when I haven't slept more than two hours and everyone is whine-crying; the days when I can't feel anything but despair and I don't even have the energy to shower but everyone's hungry; the days I shamefully wish that I could just fall asleep painlessly and never, never, ever wake up again (Does everyone have these thoughts, or is it just me?) . . . On those days, the birthdays come to me—the ones I would miss. The graduations and seasons and holidays. The childish wonder around the Christmas tree, small sandy feet jumping beach waves. My boys with teenage faces, my little girl in white on her wedding day.

I think of these things. And I realize that my children anchor me to this earth in a whole different way. They pin me down and fasten me back into life itself. They hold me steady when the storm threatens to sink me. These little lives secure me in coves of meaning, they remind me of why I live, why I have to keep living, and why it is a privilege and an honor and an unspeakable GIFT to live—yes, even when I cannot feel anything but depression's gloom.

Even the love for a child has not been enough to tether some mothers to life, however. We've read about them. Some of us knew them. And their stories make me afraid. Will my child love anchors be enough to hold me through depression's downpour?

Anchor me solidly in You, Jesus, when the tempest roars around me, and I'd just as soon disappear under its waves. You are the only Anchor that never fails.

> You have searched me, LORD, and you know me.
> You know when I sit and when I rise;
>   you perceive my thoughts from afar.
> You discern my going out and my lying down;
>   you are familiar with all my ways.
> Before a word is on my tongue
>   you, LORD, know it completely.

These words of David in Psalm 139:1–4 assure me that God is no stranger to my worst thoughts. He's quite familiar with them, discerns them all—even some before I speak them. This is comforting, and yet it's also hard, because there are some thoughts I'm ashamed I even think. He knows those too (cringe). But I find great relief when, just a few verses later, David writes, "Even the darkness will not be dark to you" (verse 12a). I know it doesn't say this, but I take that verse to mean that even *my* darkness is not too dark for Him. The deepest dungeons I have ever endured, the most dreadful considerations in my soul, are still not dark enough that He can't see through them. And if He can see through them, I believe He can bring me out of them.

I can anchor myself in that faith: that when I cannot see any possible way out, my Savior still can. It might not be something I'm able to feel. But it is something I can *choose* to believe. It is something I can cling to, with all my might.

> When my spirit grows faint within me,
>   it is you who know my way. . . .
> Set me free from my prison,
>   that I may praise your name (Psalm 142:3, 7).

Search me, God, and know my heart;
    test me and know my anxious thoughts.
See if there is any offensive way in me,
    and lead me in the way everlasting (Psalm 139:23, 24).

Anchor me deep, Jesus.
Anchor me strong.
Anchor me steadfast in You.

IN CASE YOU GET SIX MINUTES TO YOURSELF: STUDY GUIDE

1. Have you ever felt like your children are anchors holding you back? Do you feel like anything else in your life is a ball and chain you're dragging behind you?
2. When was the last time you experienced a dark depression, and what was it that anchored you into life?
3. How do we anchor ourselves in Jesus?
4. Read Psalm 139. Which verse speaks to you the most, and why?
5. Read Psalm 142, written by David when he was hiding for his life in a cave. What hope is David holding on to?
6. How strong is your anchor in Jesus today? Would it hold if suddenly a storm arose?

"Mommy, Look!"

M ommy, look!" pleads the little voice. "Look at me, Mommy! Mommy, watch me! Mommy, come *seeeeee*!"

If I could erase just one phrase from motherhood, it would be the phrase: "Mommy, look!" I know that sounds terrible. I realize this phrase is not a bombastic order barked by demanding tyrants, though it feels that way. It's really just a sweet, innocent invitation to be part of a moment that my child finds meaningful. I get it. It's just . . . I can't take it anymore.

"Mommy, look!" gets shouted at me during the very worst times throughout the day: in the middle of the dinner rush, while I'm on the phone with the bank, as I'm merging onto a crowded freeway, or even while I'm in the shower. My little drill sergeants insist on my attention when I'm engrossed in a task, unable to respond, and even when I'm asleep. "Mommy, *psssst* . . . wake up, Mommy, *look*!" stage-whispers slither through my cracked bedroom door.

It's not that I don't want to look (well, OK, sometimes I really don't). Most of the time I want to see them. I enjoy watching them. I love to observe their achievements and share in their special moments with them. I desire to make them feel noticed, important, and valued. To be honest, I can even admit that I'm honored they still ask me. There will come a day when they won't give one hoot whether I'm looking or not, and probably will prefer that I *don't*! So I value this phrase, I do. But I've also come to dread it.

The simple fact is that I just want to do a chore without being interrupted. That's it. Just one task—one opportunity—to finish what I started, is really all I want. But I get it—they love for me to be a part of their happy moments. They want me to see them.

I guess I want this same thing from God. I want Him to look. I want Him to be watching me. I want Him to notice me when I'm at my best or as I'm doing good deeds. I'm proud for Him to see when I've been a good wife or patiently taught my child an important lesson. I delight in the knowledge that He's enjoying some of the happiest moments of our lives right along with us.

But I think I want Him to see me even more during the hard times. When I'm bitter or blue, heartsick and hurting—it's in these times that I really *need* to know He sees me, because I need to know He cares. I long to feel important to Him, to know His nearness, sense His comfort. "Father, *look*," I plead. "Just let me know that You're paying attention, assure me that You're here, that You can see me." When everyone around me seems to be basking in God's blessings, and yet I can't even catch a glimpse of Him, it's then I need to know that He still glimpses me.

Lots of people throughout the Bible have given God grand and glorious names, but perhaps I like Hagar's name for God best of all. Impregnated by Abraham—likely against her will—and then violently mistreated by Sarah, her mistress, Hagar flees into the desert seemingly alone. But she is not alone. The angel of the Lord finds her, tells her she's having a son, gives her his name, details his future, and then tells her to return to Sarah. After hearing all of this, Hagar states plainly, "You are the God who sees me." In a time when the gods were considered distant and unconcerned with human life, Hagar has found a God intimate enough to discern her story, perceive her thoughts, examine her future, and instill her with a new vision. This homeless, pagan, Egyptian-born servant discovered the God who sees.

I still remember the exact second when Caleb realized he was lost—panic spread across his face, followed by a look of sheer terror, and he scanned the crowds in all directions for me. It was the Fourth of July holiday, and we had gathered on a large field with friends to watch a fireworks display. Caleb decided to wander off toward the playground in search of his friends, and after a few minutes of watching him from my place on the picnic blanket, I decided I would purchase some popcorn before the lines grew too long. I headed toward the vendors, but I still kept an eye on Caleb in the crowd.

He didn't know this, however. After crossing the monkey bars and chasing his friends around the slides, he turned back to look for me, and I was gone. I watched him begin to run back and forth in confusion, crying and yelling, "Mommy! Mommy!" through the throngs of people. He couldn't see me. He thought I had left him. He was fearful that he was abandoned and alone in this sea of strangers. But the whole time, I was watching.

From the very second I saw that horror cross his face, I began making my way over to him. While he ran the wrong direction in search of our blanket, I followed him. When he stopped a nearby fireman in full uniform and insisted he was lost, I had almost reached him. And when I finally scooped him up in my arms, one big mess of tears and fears and relief, I assured him over and over through his sobs, "Mommy was watching you, honey! Mommy could see you! I never even took my eyes off you, my boy. Mommy saw you feeling lost the entire time."

I have been so lost that I became certain God no longer saw me. I've experienced fears so immense and disappointments so deep that I've cried out in terror, "Where are You?" and then in anger, "Where are You!" The unanswered prayers. The silences. The sickness and loss. I have felt invisible to God.

But how I feel is not the truest thing, in the end. Because through it all, from the very first moment I started to feel lost, He saw me. He pursued me. Perhaps He was making His way toward me even as I resented His absence, but I just didn't know it. Sometimes we have to cling to what we know above what we can feel. And according to the Bible, what we can know for sure is that God is a God who sees. He sees me. He sees you. He sees everything. While we are trying desperately to get His attention, trying everything we can think of to make Him just "Look, Father, look!" He is already on His way to find us.

IN CASE YOU GET SIX MINUTES TO YOURSELF: STUDY GUIDE

1. What is the one constantly repeated phrase that you'd like to strike from the record of motherhood forever?
2. Did you ever get lost as a kid? Have any of your children ever been lost? What did that feel like?
3. Read the full story of Hagar in Genesis 16, and then later in Genesis 21:8–21, when God finds her a second time. What is the significance of a God who both sees and hears her repeatedly? What does this teach you about God's character?
4. When is the last time you wondered whether God could see you?
5. What can Christians do when God seems distant, silent, or "lost"?
6. How would you or how have you explained God's silence to your children? To yourself?
7. In what ways do you need "the God who sees" today?

Stones

"Daddy, why do you have a broken old brick on this shelf?" my son asked on a family garage cleaning day in early spring. "It's got stuff in the middle of it, and this side is black. Is it from the olden days? Are you gonna build something with it?"

I looked up from the box of baby clothes I was sorting. My husband, Greg, put down the stack of boards he was piling. We looked at our boy Toby, we looked at the brick, and then our eyes met. Yep. It was the one.

"That's a very special brick, sweetie," I began. "That's from the fire."

"You mean when your house burned down?" he wondered. "At Auburn? *That* fire?"

"It wasn't just our house," Greg explained. "It was the entire dorm—the whole building. Mommy was one of the girls' deans, so we were living inside the dorm when it caught on fire."

"Do you remember the story?" I asked Toby hopefully. "Do you remember what happened?"

"Yeah," he assured me, "I remember, Mommy. You lost all your things and your clothes and books and plates and everything. Even your tea and teapots, Mommy. Everything."

We laughed. Did I say I lost teapots, or is he just assuming he knows what would have been in my house before he was born?

"And you had to eat McDonald's for dinner and for breakfast the next day because the people that worked there felt sorry for you about the fire and brought a giant box," older brother Caleb added matter-of-factly.

I love learning which details stand out to them.

"But why did you keep this old brick, Mommy?" Toby needed to know.

"Well, to remember, honey," I explained. "When the big machines tore the building apart after the fire, the working men asked everyone if we wanted to keep a brick. And Mommy decided to keep one because I wanted to always have something that reminds me of the fire, in case many years pass and I don't think about it anymore."

"How come you want to remember something so bad, Mommy?" Caleb looked disturbed.

I paused. How to explain? Seeing my hesitation, Greg asked the boys, "Do you boys know how many of the eighty-six girls that Mommy took care of in that building got hurt? Did any of them get burned or trapped or die in the fire?"

"Nope!" they both cried, "Nobody, Daddy!" Caleb said, "Jesus helped everybody to make it out OK! Even the man who went in later to check if there were girls stuck in there, Jesus even saved him in a special *biiiiiiig* way!" He gestured with his hands to show just how big.

It touches and amazes me to hear them recount this event in their own words.

"Mommy feels so thankful for that, boys. And even though Mommy was really, really sad to lose all her things, it makes Mommy so happy to know that all of those girls are alive today, somewhere out there in the world, starting families and having adventures, and living happy lives."

"So you keep this brick to remember them?" Younger son Toby was still trying to understand.

I took the brick from his little hands, rough yellow stone smeared with fire's ash. A stampede of memories charged through my mind. Faces. Voices. Arms. The ringing of alarms, the shrill sirens. Rosters of names. The cheer when all were accounted for. Sour smoke-smell in our clothes and hair. The thunderous crash of the roof falling in. Red-hot flames leaping against the black November night sky. It's so hard to sum up in a single explanation.

"I keep this brick," I began, "to remember what Jesus did for us."

I looked at them both. I waited.

"Mommy hasn't thought about that fire in a long time," I admitted, "probably not for many months now. It was ten years ago. So when I don't think about the fire, I don't think about how Jesus saved us either. It's not that I forget it; I just don't think about it every day. But then one day, when I see this brick on the shelf, I remember to think about it, and I remember to thank Jesus. But the best part is that I remember to tell you the story again. Because it's an important story to Mommy."

They both nodded their heads. They seemed satisfied. Caleb took the brick out of my hands then and placed it back up on the shelf, pushing everything else aside for about twelve inches in both directions.

"For you can see it easier, Mommy," he said, "and *always* remember."

There are a lot of memorials that my husband and I have tried to incorporate into our family life. We observe natural memorials like holidays and seasons, of course. Family memorials like birthdays, moving days, and anniversaries are celebrated with as much festivity as we can muster. But we've tried to add others in as well. Like last year on Memorial Day, when we helped the boys call my ninety-two-year-old grandpa and thank him for serving in the navy on the USS *Dixie* in World War II. When the day comes in October that our faithful yellow lab Summer lost her battle to cancer, we look at pictures of her and share our favorite stories about things she did. Each year on my children's birthdays, I try to tell them something new about the day they were born. On the yearly anniversary of the first date my husband ever took me on (a spontaneous walk through the Sunken Gardens in Lincoln, Nebraska, in the rain), we take the whole family walking through a local garden together, rain or shine. And every year on November 17 (the day of the Auburn Adventist Academy fire), we tell stories, show the recorded news footage, and then we go eat at McDonald's—to remember, to give thanks, and to celebrate life.

All of us have memorials like this—days and dates we observe, traditions we've woven into the fabric of our families because we want to honor something, someone, or some time we've passed through. Most people probably wouldn't keep an old brick, I admit. But everyone has their "thing." I know a family who throws birthday parties every year on the day their children were dedicated to the Lord. Another friend of mine celebrates "gotcha day"—the day she adopted her daughter from China. The events we observe differ just as much as we do, but whether they're silly or serious, we're all invested in them, one way or another.

God is pretty invested in memorials too.

When the people of Israel crossed the rolled-back rapids of the Jordan River on dry ground, God asked Joshua to do something specific. "Choose twelve men from among the people, from each tribe, and tell them to take up twelve stones from the middle of the Jordan," He instructed. "And carry them over with you and put them down at the place where you stay tonight" (Joshua 4:2, 3). When the stone-bearers reached the banks, they heaved these massive stones all the way into Gilgal, where they camped. There, Joshua set them up to form a memorial of the crossing, and it was recorded in the book's writing that "they are there to this day" (verse 9).

But what's more significant than the memorial itself is what God asks them to do for their kids. "[Joshua] said to the Israelites, 'In the future when your descendants ask their parents, "What do these stones mean?" tell them, "Israel crossed the Jordan on dry ground." For the LORD your God dried up the Jordan before you until you had crossed over. The LORD your God did to the Jordan what he had done to the Red Sea when he dried it up before us until we had crossed over. He did this so that all the peoples of the earth might know that the hand of the LORD is powerful and so that you might always fear the LORD your God' " (verse 21–24). Many years later, when their children found the odd pile of stones and asked, "Mommy, Daddy, are these from the olden days? Are you gonna build something with them?" the parents were transported back in time. They suddenly remembered the struggle to push ox carts through riverbed sand, recalled the water foaming in the distance, and relived the excitement of finally crossing into the Promised Land.

I believe that we are still called to do this today—to collect bricks. Set up stones. Record memorials of what God has done and tell the stories every chance we get. It's easy to accept God's blessings with gratitude when they happen and then move on and forget about them altogether. That's why we need to be intentional about putting reminders into our lives that we return to, year after year. We've got to get good at sneaking these stories into any old random day.

Why? Because this is one of the most important ways that faith is passed on. Through our stories, the seeds of our children's beliefs are planted, tended, rooted, and brought to maturity, and so are our own. One day, should our kids find themselves questioning whether God is even real, they will remember our stories, and the stories will build an altar of evidence that they can cling to. One day, should we find *ourselves* questioning whether God is real or where He has gone to and why He is so distant, those stories become the lifeboats that sail us through the storm.

God knows our children will find the bricks on our back shelves. He anticipated them asking about imposing piles of stones. So let's pack our lives full of what God has done. Let's tell and tell and tell again the stories of how He's led us, how He's blessed us, how He's seen us through. Let's seize every opportunity available to share an old salvation tale.

"Let this be written for a future generation, that a people not yet created may praise the LORD" (Psalm 102:18).

IN CASE YOU GET SIX MINUTES TO YOURSELF: STUDY GUIDE

1. What keepsakes or traditions do you have that remind you and your family of a special person or event?
2. Read the story of the Israelites crossing the Jordan in Joshua 3 and 4. Does this sound like an event they were likely to forget? Why were the stones needed?
3. What does it mean to set up "memorials" in our lives of what God has done? How, specifically, can we do this?
4. When have you been certain of God's activity and involvement in your life? Have you ever told these stories? How significant do they become to you in dark times?
5. How do our stories solidify our faith? Our children's faith? What other opportunities can we use to pass faith on?
6. What story are you in the middle of living right now, and how is God making Himself known to you?

Batman

My three-year-old son honestly believes with all his heart that when he puts on his Batman costume, he himself suddenly morphs into the real, true Batman. I haven't ever questioned him about the facts of how this incarnation takes place because, honestly, I don't want him to think about it too hard. I love it that he believes this, and I don't want to challenge him out of it.

It is hard to explain why, but I have somehow come to depend on Batman. So many dreary mornings I have taken courage in the sight of a little mini superhero suddenly appearing around the corner of the hallway. Batman shows up in the kitchen to help with the cooking just when I start to feel lonely. The caped crusader cheerfully meets the mailman at the door when my hands are too full of babies or burdens to answer the door. And on so many countless mornings and afternoons, silent Batman sits faithfully beside me while I nurse one or the other of the twins to sleep. In short, Batman comes to spice up life just when life needs a little spicing.

I think Batman found his muse and mission in our home this year precisely because of the arrival of the twin babies. Instantly not the family's youngest any longer, I suspect Toby decided he needed a new way to captivate the family's attention (though with his quick wit, brilliant imagination, and insanely creative humor, he most certainly already did). I have noticed that there is a particular pattern to when Batman shows up. It is usually when Toby himself needs a little "help."

Batman peers down shyly from the stairs when unknown new guests arrive at the door, giving the little boy inside courage to face the strangers. Batman bursts in when I've been particularly busy, preoccupied, or absent, making his entrance with the kind of gusto a mommy just simply cannot ignore. And Batman urgently rescues his toys from the deadly clutches of the Joker whenever stress or anger are running high in the house all around him. With a keen eye for impending danger, my little Batman comes whenever someone is flashing the help signal in the sky.

Tonight—two days unshowered, covered in kids' throw-up, and kicking the laundry heap at my feet—I am wishing I could become Batman too. Or Batgirl, or Wonder Woman, or someone or something or anything that would lift me out of my reality for just a little while. I wish I had a costume that gave me the courage to face life's difficulties. I wish I had an alter ego to make me better, stronger, and wiser than I am. Mostly, I just wish there was a better version of me out there.

Sometimes on nights like tonight, I randomly get flashbacks of myself ten years ago as a girls' dean of eighty-six adolescents. I recall with wonder the cocky, self-assured way I approached absolutely everything in life. Where did that come from? Where is it now? And *why* was raising other people's kids so much easier? If I open old yearbooks, I can read tributes from so many students about how I "changed their lives," "strengthened their faith," and even "led them to Jesus." Who was that girl my old students wrote to? I have to forcefully make myself believe that she was in fact me, because tonight I don't feel I have the power to change the wet laundry from the washer to the dryer, let alone change anyone's life. I cannot fathom strengthening anyone's faith, because my own faith is kicking for dear life to keep its head above water. And if I somehow manage to lead my children to Jesus in spite of all my unforgivable mistakes and gut-wrenching failings, I will be amazed. Dumbfounded and speechless, for lack of an explanation.

That is why I'm up wishing for a Batsuit. (That, and the fact that I just emptied another bowl of throw-up, maybe for the fourteenth time today.) And the easy conclusion is that no matter how much laundry I manage to excavate this family from, I will never find my supersuit. That idealized version of me won't turn up at the bottom of any toy basket or beneath any pile of dishes either.

However.

Beside me sits another type of armor—one battle worn, tested, tried, and true. Late-night lamplight reflects off my two-toned leather-covered Bible and my smooth red prayer journal underneath. You cannot imagine the extent to which these two companions have saved me (or maybe you can). I would be horrified for you to read the journal's blubbering pages, but if you did, what you would find there is a record of a girl crying out to God for help. Begging over and over for more patience, more wisdom. Pleading for strength, courage, and love. Confessing unthinkable shortcomings. Asking Him on every page just exactly how I am supposed to mold and shape these tiny little characters for His kingdom when I myself am such a mess. And then, after pages of these desperate pleas and rantings, almost always there will come an answer: a tiny psalm, a succinct verse, scribbled out in haste from memory—a puzzle piece snapped into place.

"My strength is made perfect in weakness."

"Be still, and know that I am God."

"Never will I leave you, never will I forsake you."

"Our God is a fortress."

"Even the darkness is not dark to me."

"He gently leads those that have young."

"If any of you lacks wisdom, he should ask God, who gives generously to all."

"Come unto me, all you who are weary [and throw-up] laden."

"I can do all things through Christ who strengthens me."

These quoted words from underlined favorite passages in my Bible are the closest I think I'll ever come to a supersuit. But they do the job—they give me courage to face the unknown and companionship for the dark days. They fill me with fervor to fight the bad guys out there who undoubtedly are after my children's souls. They remind me that salvation for my family never resided in my own hands anyway, but rested completely in His scarred hands all along. And they fortify me in the way that only living and active words from an ever-present God could. They change me, grow me, and strengthen me in all the threadbare spots of my worn-out mommy soul. They are my supersuit. They really *do* have the power to make me more than I am. (Holy ancient words, Batman!)

I wish I was better about keeping this armor on. I yearn to be more consistent in my time with the Lord, and I wish that He didn't lose the competition for my time so often to sleep (or Facebook). But when things get bad enough—as they always will in motherhood—I eventually do remember there is an unlimited source of power ever at my disposal.

And so, I keep coming back for more. Late at night when the rest of the house sleeps and snores, I am here thirsting at this well that never runs dry. Basking in the intimacy of being completely known and yet still somehow completely loved. Finding my courage. Finding my joy again. Finding my own original Batman: "the Lord is a Warrior—He is mighty to save."

IN CASE YOU GET SIX MINUTES TO YOURSELF: STUDY QUESTIONS

1. For which situations in your life right now would you most like to have a super-suit or superpower?
2. Where do you habitually go when you realize you are not enough?
3. Which passages of Scripture have brought you the most comfort over the years? Which bring you the most comfort today?
4. Is it true that we can wear the words of the Lord like armor? How and why would this work? What could this do for you in motherhood?
5. Where are you most threadbare and thirsty today, and how do the Scriptures speak to your particular situation?

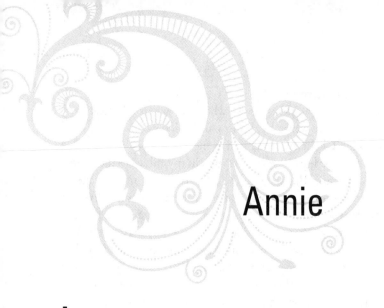

Annie

Is it possible to prepare for the moment you think you're watching your child die? As he fell from ten feet above, over the old-fashioned slide's thin metal edge, Caleb let out one single heart-stopping scream. His little head and back slapped the ground with a violent thud, and then he lay motionless as a rag doll. His eyes rolled back in his head, taking on the stare of the dead. His face turned a pale gray. And he stopped breathing.

Rewind about ten years, to my college-self schlepping into Emergency Health Care class on a snowy, late February afternoon. As ever, the plastic dummies we'd randomly named "Annie" were sprawled in various positions around the classroom. Daily we dropped our bags at our desks, chose a faceless victim, and began the same exact routine:

Dropping to our knees. Shaking the body. "Annie, Annie, are you OK?" No response. Annie was never OK.

Turning to a make-believe partner and commanding, "Help! Call 911!"

Tilting the head, checking for breathing—cheek against nose to be sure and feel it, in case it was so light it couldn't be seen. Annie was never breathing.

Warm lips covering plastic mouth, pumping two deep breaths into Annie's lifeless waiting cavern.

When her chest rose—evidence that the breaths hit home—then two fingers found her jugular and searched for a pulse. Annie never had a pulse.

And so the chest compressions and varied breathing rounds of CPR would commence, on and on, until at some point the teacher would declare, "OK, that's good, everyone; let's begin class."

Every day we did this in Emergency Health Care class—every single day.

But on that February day, after almost eight weeks of repeating this mind-numbing cycle time and time again, I just couldn't take it anymore. I stood defiantly in the center of the room and raised my voice in protest to the professor. "*Why* do we have to keep doing this?" I demanded. "We know this stuff already; this is ridiculous! I'm so tired of it! There's no reason to keep doing this over and over like stupid robots." I was bold back then, apparently.

The teacher met me with an even gaze, and confidence crossed her stormy blue eyes as she declared, "There is a reason to do this over and over, Melissa." Then, turning to address the room, she said, "Listen up, class. Melissa wants to know why we keep repeating this predictable pattern, so I'm going to tell you why." She looked right at me then, and still to this day I can recite what she said: "I want you to know this so well, so instinctively, so intuitively, that should you ever find yourself in a situation where you really have to use it, you won't even hesitate. You won't pause, you won't question yourself, you won't stop to think. Because it will be automatic." I dropped my eyes in defeat, realizing this was an argument I wouldn't win. "I'm drilling this into you, class, so that it will be with you for life."

Nobody dared say a word. Several heads nodded. We all accepted our fate, and the class resumed as normal. I slunk to the corner and asked Annie whether she was OK (she wasn't). We continued to complete this exercise for the rest of the semester—another two long months of saving poor plastic Annie. When the class was finally over, I rejoiced that I would never have to see old Annie again.

And then I forgot about her. During the summer I was a waterfront lifeguard, during the early mornings at the college pool, I never once had to use my CPR training, thank God. I left college, went on to become a mother, and didn't think of Annie a day in my life.

Until his body hit the ground. Until my own son, my first child, lay motionless, the look of death on his face. I saw the scene play out from a park bench where I was sitting nearby, big-bellied and eight months pregnant with my second son. When his head hit, something funny happened to time: it stood suspended, it came to a stop. Nothing felt quite real. But do you know what I did that day?

I jumped up from the bench and ran to my baby boy, pregnant tummy and all, and dropped to my knees beside him on the ground.

Without thinking, without crying, without even so much as a single hesitation, I shook him softly and said, "Caleb, Caleb, are you OK?" Caleb did not respond. Caleb was not OK.

"Help!" I turned to my husband. "Call 911 immediately, tell them what happened!"

I tenderly tilted my son's head, chin up, and checked for breathing, cheek against nostrils to be able to feel even the slightest sign. Caleb was not breathing.

At this point, I had the fleeting thought that I might be watching my own child die before my very eyes, but the idea came and went as I pressed my warm lips over his cold ones, filled his precious little lungs with two pumps of my very own air. I watched his chest rise, this tiny chest I held against my skin on the day he was born, and knew the breaths had hit home.

My fingers found their way down the curve of his jaw, to his jugular, to a small but steady pulse. His heart—it was working! But he still was not breathing.

I would breathe for him, I knew, as long as I had breath. Warm lips covering gray motionless ones again, sending much-needed air into the little cavity. I counted breaths per minute, stopped to check his pulse, and kept breathing when I found it still with us. I breathed, and I breathed, and I breathed into his little mouth. I didn't stop. I didn't question myself. Just kept breathing, watching, counting, pulse-checking, breathing, watching, counting, pulse-checking, and breathing. I lost track of the number of cycles—maybe I had done seven, maybe twenty-nine, I didn't know, but I kept breathing.

The memory of the little fingers twitching slightly beside my knees still spreads a smile across my face to this day. After his fingers lifted, his arm moved, his eyes fluttered, and then he coughed—a sputtering type of cough—and took his own first breaths. When he opened those precious deep brown eyes, my heart sang, "He's alive!" Caleb was alive. He whimpered in pain. "Don't move, sweetie," I told him calmly, "you fell a long way off that slide and you landed funny on your back. You also hit your head pretty bad. In case you broke something, Mommy needs you to stay very, very still, OK?"

"OK, Mommy," he whined, "but Caleb has owies!" *Caleb has owies,* I thought, *but Caleb will live.*

It wasn't until we were at the hospital, standing in the hallway outside the lab where Caleb underwent X-rays from every angle imaginable that I started to cry. The full weight of what had just happened fell on me at last, and I experienced all the frantic thoughts, all the paralyzing fear and self-doubt that waited obediently behind habit's dam. Greg wrapped his arms around me sideways, over the baby bulge, as I broke down sobbing. He held me quietly at first. Then he whispered into my hair, "Honey, I was so proud of you today. You saved our boy. You just got down there and did it without even thinking—you didn't even panic like you normally would! How did you even know how to do that?"

One thought alone appeared in my head: *Annie.* Then and only then did I remember my lessons with old Annie. And my teacher's words came flooding back to me then, drenched in all-new meaning and emotion: "I want you to know this so well that if you ever have to use it someday, you won't even think. It will just be automatic." It was, I realized. It was automatic, it was in me, just as she said. I didn't even have to think. I don't remember thinking *anything,* I just knelt down beside him and began rescue breathing.

What I really want to know now, here in these motherhood years, is how to train my heart to turn to Jesus automatically like this, when life's emergencies burst in unexpected. How do I program myself to drop to my knees and breathe in His life-giving presence instead of hesitating, panicking, turning away, or filling with fear? Those are the natural responses of a sin-defiant heart, but they aren't the ones I want. I want a mind trained so systematically in faith that I know exactly what to do when the crisis comes. When I'm spinning out of control across a crowded freeway, when I answer that phone call in the night, when I get that test result back from the hospital, when depression drapes its dreaded darkness over me—I want to turn to Jesus without even thinking. I want it to be the most natural response on earth. How can I make sure that I react this way?

And how can I teach my children to do this too? When their ingrained responses are anger, jealousy, and revenge, how do I tutor them to choose God's ways instead?

The answer lies again with Annie, of course: practice. Daily, consistent, repetitive practice, over and over, in the mundane moments. Constant lessons in guiding ourselves and our children back to Jesus.

It's too late to train our hearts when the emergency comes; the crisis will only reveal what we already have inside of us. When we get lost in doubt, that's really not the time to build faith; we have to rely on the faith we've already constructed. When we are overcome by sadness or fear, it's not the easiest moment to learn of the Lord's goodness. We must already have the assurance of His love if we are to believe in its existence even when we can't see one bit of evidence for it at all. When our children are boiling mad at baby brother, that isn't always the opportunity to educate on forgiveness. Forgiveness has to be instilled, demonstrated, and prepared ahead of time. We must discipline ourselves instead during the safe times, recite His faithfulness over and over again, in the classrooms of everyday life.

Sometimes I think about the giants of faith in the Bible. Old Daniel, his tired legs hobbling up the steps to his room, wrinkled hands opening the windows toward Jerusalem. With the death threat hanging fresh in the air, Daniel still publicly bows his head and prays to his God. Was he afraid? Was he crazy? Why did he do this? Wouldn't a closed closet have worked just as well that day? No—Daniel knew that to not appear in his window as always would communicate fear and defeat. Faith was part of his practice, part of his daily rhythm, and he would not be deprived of it for any reason.

It would be easy to write off Daniel as a special situation, but there are so many others who echo his ways. Shadrach, Meshach, and Abednego standing before the golden statue, refusing to bow down, fiery furnace radiating heat behind them—this wasn't the day their faith developed. When Paul and Silas sang hymns in a jail cell as their bleeding blisters oozed, this wasn't the moment they discovered joy. David's courage didn't appear on the battlefield as Goliath advanced, it had been cultivated silently among the sheep. Jesus didn't hang on the cross surrounded by God's presence—we know that was taken away from Him, hidden from reach. Separated from the Father for the first time in eternity's history, left to shoulder sin's crushing weight alone, Jesus leaned by faith on the unfelt assurance that His Father still loved Him. "Into thy hands I commend my spirit," He whispered hoarsely as He died in complete lack of that Spirit's presence, still faithful to the end (Luke 23:46, KJV). We have hope today because Jesus knew exactly what to do in an emergency.

There are so many things in motherhood that I wish were automatic—such as having patience, for example, or knowing the right answers. I wish that I automatically knew how to grow my children's faith or that I automatically understood how to instill core values. The truth is, I don't. But instead of beating myself up for this lack of knowledge, I'm guiding myself to seek Jesus instead. I know that I cannot be prepared for the real emergencies that loom in the future, but He is. He can see them, He knows them already. And because He's the great Teacher, He faithfully calls me—day after day after day—"Come, child, come and prepare with Me. I don't want you to panic when the terror arrives. I want My assurance to be rooted in you, automatically and without hesitation, laid down repeatedly during a hundred small lessons of turning to Me."

Mommies, may we be intentional about practicing faith in the mundane moments, and may we search for ways to specifically show our children this secret as well. Like the heroes of old, we, too, must be skilled in schooling our hearts to habitually turn to Jesus. Let's commit to coaching our kids and ourselves to seek Him in small situations so that we are ready and equipped to seek Him in the big ones.

Develop this steadfastness in me, My Father. Teach my wandering soul to turn to You daily, hourly, in any of the myriad small "emergencies" that crop up in life. I want to be prepared so that, should I ever need to fall on You in a real emergency, my heart will be trained—it will already automatically know what to do. Call me, Great Teacher, ever back to Your classroom.

IN CASE YOU GET SIX MINUTES TO YOURSELF: STUDY GUIDE

1. Have you ever had the experience of thinking you were watching your child die? Have you ever been terrified enough to question whether his or her actual life was in danger?
2. What were the habits that your teachers, pastors, and parents endeavored to instill in you regularly during your youth and childhood? Are these habits still with you today?
3. Read the story of Daniel facing the threat of the lions' den in Daniel chapter 6. What are the specific signs and phrases that hint at how steadfast Daniel's prayer life really was? What can you learn from this man of faith?
4. What are some practical ways you can begin training your children to turn to Jesus in the small moments? Is there anything you can do in the big moments?
5. What are some practical ways you can reinforce your own soul's routine of turning to Jesus?
6. In which area of your life do you need to turn to Jesus today? Are there any areas in which you have been purposely turning away from Him? What do you need to do about these?

Ten Things I Hate About You, Motherhood

(and a Bunch of Other Stuff I Simply Adore)

1. Syrup

I liked syrup before I had children, I really did. It was sweet sugary goodness. But then I had kids, and the kids ate syrup just this one time only, and now it is somehow all over each and every surface and piece of furniture and clothing item we own. And it's invisible to the naked eye, just like disease. So it sits waiting on my table until I lay down that very important paper and only *then* does it show itself. Really, I don't understand its magical powers . . . It travels straight from plate to mouth via fork, yet somehow it multiplies onto eyebrows and ankles and curtains? Unbelievable.

2. Poop

Nothing in life is constant besides death and taxes—and poop. Motherhood is one big long stretch of dealing with other humans' feces many times a day. Mining poop shrapnel out of little-boy-body crevices. Cleaning poop stains out of clothes. Scrubbing poop from toilet edges, dumping poop out of plastic potty bowls, fishing floating poop out of bathtub waters, mopping poop accidents from the floor. Smelling poop. Seeing poop. Hearing poop happen from across the room. Poop is the thread that holds the fabric of each day together. Someone should write a book entitled, *Motherhood: The Poop Marathon*.

3. Bedtime

Oh bedtime, I shamefully admit to looking forward to you all day long, and yet?

I hate you. You are the hour of meltdowns and tantrums and sobbing fits. The bringer of despair. You promise cuddles and stories and goodnight kisses, yet you deliver fighting and yelling instead (and poop, of course). Why do you make all my children cry at the same time? Why do you choose this hour to deliver attitudes? And why do you morph me into the worst version of myself, on top of everything?

4. Vacations, and the lack of vacations

Vacations sound like a fabulous idea when we have children. "Take a vacation, you need it!" "Family vacations are such perfect ways to bond and create memories!" Oh yes, we will create memories all right. The kind of memories our children will be sharing from counseling couches someday. One "Mommyhood dictionary" I read offered this definition of the word *vacation:* "Trying to control your kids in a brand new location, while carting around a zillion bags of all shapes and sizes that contain your belongings. See also 'insanity.' "

The thing is, we really do need a vacation, desperately. After 1,267 days straight (but who's counting) of doing laundry and dishes and cleaning syrup and poop, we could use a break! But don't be fooled. The vacation is far more work than just simply staying at home. And the syrup and poop come with us, tenfold. Even when we try to go away without the kids, we miss them like crazy and feel guilty and miserable. They have ruined us.

5. My body

Who among us doesn't hate the stretch marks, the C-section scars, the tired breasts that nursed like slaves, the bumps and lumps in all the wrong places? This vessel has been through the war and back, and it shows. Half the time it's not even clean—we all know that nobody, *nobody* has time for a shower every single day. So we buy cute hats and twist up our hair to hide the mess, and we only post Facebook photos when we've managed to get clean and hide all the lumps under cute generous clothing. Of course, we intend to begin an exercise routine *very soon* now to take care of that . . . any day now, really . . .

6. Grocery shopping

This activity is a special kind of torture. Let me describe what it might be like for you, should you foolishly attempt it: Combine the stress of feeding a family three meals a day, seven days a week, on a very tight budget, with the madness of remembering each and every item for each meal, with the nonstop begging from your children to buy each and every piece of nonsense you pass. The children only stop begging long enough to ask for the bathroom seven times or to disappear into thin air and stop your heart. This is the stuff nightmares are made of, I'm telling you! Especially on that last little homestretch in the checkout line . . . the kids are systematically begging for every single pack of gum on display. You are praying the bill doesn't go over your budget (which it will). You are trying to shove it all back into the cart, now in bags, around children who are screaming as you yank packs of gum from their hands, while people are staring at you, judging your parenting, or telling you to "enjoy every minute!" When you finally make it out the door and start across the parking lot, swearing never to return, you remember the mayonnaise and toilet paper you forgot. But it's not worth it—just go to the car—*go*.

7. Laundry

I think laundry and syrup are related. Close cousins. They have the same amazing properties of multiplying and spreading and following me throughout all rooms of the house. I will never finish all the laundry, because what my children are wearing this instant is laundry, and likely covered in syrup or poop, or probably both. Same goes for what I am wearing. And let's not even talk about the bag of eighty-seven single socks that went into the wash as a married pair and came out widowers . . .

8. My car

I love my car! I love the design, the comfort, the power, and especially the color. My kids, however, do not love my car. And, of course, we find ourselves in this car for large unavoidable portions of every day. Each special trip begins with a deadbolt system of seatbelt security on varying makes and models of little people. The little people adamantly request little-people music that will simultaneously kill my brain cells and yet remain stuck in my brain for three weeks. The carpet is blanketed in smashed goldfish crackers and Cheerios and mismatched socks (Aha!), and the seat contents resemble a lost-and-found bin at a baseball game. And there is that dirty diaper smell coming from . . . somewhere . . .

9. Phone calls

It's the highlight in an otherwise mundane day of drudgery—the phone lighting up with the name of the exact friend I've been longing to hear from! Hooray! Another adult is contacting me from the outside world! Suddenly, my heart is full of so much to say and share, but no—I've gotten ahead of myself. I won't be sharing anything. I'll be cleaning up the broken glass off the floor or desperately searching for Band-Aids while someone is shrieking and bleeding. I'll be interrupted every two minutes. Every disaster that was scheduled for the week will instead happen right now, during this phone call. Except for the one that bedtime is saving—don't forget about that one.

10. Church

I know I'm supposed to love church (I used to, I try to . . .), and I hope that one day my kids grow up to love church. But right now, it's an exercise in futility. I have to wake myself and my children way earlier than usual, so everyone begins the day crabby. We have to wear nice clothes—clean nice clothes—which means laundry planning. And they have to be quiet for more than an hour. No amount of quiet toys or fruit snacks or magnet games can fill up an hour. But an hour is short enough for everyone to "need" to visit the drinking fountain three times and to have a sneezing fit and a head-turning argument, and to grind fruit snacks into the carpet in front of me approximately every eleven inches. And to color all over the nice Sabbath clothes, and throw a toy car directly into the neck of the lady in front of us. Oh—and to have one high-speed race down the aisle. Why did I come to church again—to hear something—a sermon maybe? I thought I would actually get twenty straight minutes of uninterrupted quiet time? That's cute.

11. Not sleeping

I don't even need to explain this one. You haven't slept a full night in twenty-one months either, and just the sight of the word *sleep* on the page made you physically ache . . . I know, I know. You're so sleep deprived and so exhausted, you didn't even notice I added an extra complaint to this list of ten. It's OK. Go take a rest. (Oh, wait, someone is pooping . . .)

Things that almost made the list, but not quite: plastic toys, singing toys, broken toys, Lego blocks, becoming the referee for every single fight and argument, the dreaded phrase, "Mommy, can I help?" and the ever-incessant phrase, "Mommy, *look*!"

Well, now I've complained. A lot. And we all know it isn't nice to complain. In fact, when my children complain, I make them think of two nice things to say instead. So I guess it's time to say some nice things about motherhood. OK. Here goes.

Some things I absolutely adore about motherhood

1. Bedtime

I know, it's cheating to have bedtime on the "love" list because I first put it on the "hate" list—but really, I recommend this: stand by your child's crib/bed and watch them sleep. Gaze on the relaxed cherub faces and follow the little chests as they rise and fall, rise and fall. It is motherhood's best elixir. See if your heart doesn't suddenly want to burst with love and pride and the desire to throw open the windows and proclaim to the neighborhood, "I made these perfect human beings! See how radiant and angelic they are?" (Ah, why didn't I see it when they were stabbing each other with forks at dinner time?)

2. My body

Yeah, I'm cheating again—this was also on the hate list. But I have to admit—immediately after I cringe at the dark ugly line of my C-section scar, I usually feel something remarkably akin to pride. My twins came into the world through that scar, and without it, we all three would have died. Scars say "I survived." And to me they say, "I made two humans at the same time—wow—I am *awesome*." I also kind of chuckle at my hips that are off-kilter from always having carried my babies on the left side. They remind me that I am adaptable. And the lumps and bumps—well, would I trade my children to get back the firm, toned body I (can claim that I) had before them? Not a chance. If I switch perspectives, those lumps can remind me just how very lucky I truly have been in this life.

3. Not sleeping

Just kidding. Nothing could make me love that. Nothing.

And I'm done stealing from the first list, so, the real number 3 goes to . . .

3. Snuggles

I can't think of too many things on earth that are more wonderful than a calm child curled up in my lap, a just-woken baby nestling into my neck, or a miniature warm body snuggled up beside me in bed on a gray, rainy morning. Snuggles are the best—the highlights of motherhood. The extra paychecks. The reason we endure the drudgery and the mess and the syrup and poop. And for me, it's worth it—when my arms are wrapped around my precious ones, every hassle I've had to face that day seems small compared to the privilege of having and loving them. Any time one of my children sits still long enough for me to hold them, I feel as though time slows down. I rest my nose on the top of their head, breathe in the smell of their hair, rub my cheeks against that perfect skin of theirs, and usually well up with joy and gratitude for being their mommy.

4. Holidays

It's hard to find words to describe the magic of seeing Fourth of July fireworks reflecting in the eyes of barefoot boys on hot July nights. Or to capture the feeling of wonder and joy on Christmas morning as they dance around in their pajamas with glee beside the tree. I loved holidays as a child, but as a mommy, getting to relive holidays through the eyes of my children is priceless. I think I am more excited than they are for Easter egg hunts and fall party costumes. When I watch grubby, fat baby hands smash pumpkin pie into their mouths for the very first taste, it's better than eating pie myself. The festivity of keeping them up till midnight on New Year's Eve, the heart-stopping Valentine's cards they design for me themselves with so much love and pride—who doesn't delight in these moments? Looking around the table during Thanksgiving dinner and realizing that I am blessed beyond measure—nobody can put a price tag on this, and I honestly wouldn't trade them for anything in all the world.

5. Seasons

This one is a bit similar to holidays, except that seasons can hold their own joy on any old random, unremarkable day of the week. I love watching my children jumping waves at the beach or splashing in the backyard kiddie pool. I adore the myriads of colorful fall leaves that they bring to me faithfully as gifts every autumn, or the bouquets of spring dandelions they collected from the grass. I have to use the word *magical* again here, and it is—it is magical to lie under the summer night sky, shoulder to shoulder, waiting and wishing for shooting stars. And it's beyond magical—it is epic—to hear their squeals of delight when they wake up to the first snowfall of the season. Some of my favorite moments of motherhood have revolved around the changing of the seasons: discovering blue robin's eggshells fallen from the apple trees, running out into a crisp autumn evening to catch sight of the geese flying south overhead, dancing in the spring rain, or swimming in lakes in summertime with the weight of tiny arms around my neck. All the things I love about the changing seasons become even more wonderful when I get to share them with my kids.

6. Family worship

Worship is different from church because you can come in your pajamas with your unwashed hair and your sticky syrup hands (and arms and legs and feet), and nobody will look at your kids like they're the poor kids. My children sing and dance around the living room like hoodlums with such joy on their faces. Or they huddle around while stories of the ages are shared. It's an amazing feeling to tell them a Bible story for the first time—to be there the moment they learn about strong Samson or Balaam's talking donkey. I also always marvel at how much truth gets spoken in prayer. I learn their loves, victories, and their worries—things that I otherwise likely wouldn't have taken the time to ask about. OK, and I have to admit that when one of my restless little boys suddenly tunes in to the story I'm reading and exclaims, "Hey! We learned about this at church!" I feel thankful for church. There's an entire community of faith investing in my children, and I'm not in this alone. I'm grateful for that. (Just not the herding cats part of it.)

7. Their darling clothes (but not socks)

How I love their clothes—infant-sized sparkly ballet slippers, tiny boy denim overalls, sun bonnets with long trailing bows, and creepy-crawly bug rain boots. They are all just so stinkin' cute! I adore dressing my boys in suits and clip-on ties because they look like miniature little men, and sometimes I think I can see the men they might become. I relish the time each day when I get to choose matching hair bows and socks for my daughter's outfits. Whether I loved dressing dolls as a girl, I don't remember, but what I know for sure is that my kiddos are my real live dolls for now, and I love it.

8. Watching them change and grow

I was tempted to put this one on the hate list, because change is hard for me. I get sad when they grow out of those adorable overalls or bonnets, and I get sentimental when they suddenly say a baby-talk word in clear English. It's easy to mourn each precious moment as it goes. But it's also amazing to see them turning into real people with quirky personalities, endearing traits, remarkable intelligence, and unforgettable creativity. I love watching their stories unfold as they go about the business of becoming who they will become. I love the honor of being a part of those stories too.

9. Play

I'm not good at playing anymore. I have forgotten so much from my childhood, but mostly how to relax, imagine, and not take myself so seriously. My kids are re-teaching me how to play, and I love it. Huddled behind the shower curtain trying not to breathe, with my heart pounding in anticipation of being found, I remember what it was like to be a kid playing hide-and-seek on rainy days. They are reminding me of the joy of building blanket forts and the value in skipping rocks. I had forgotten how much I love to climb trees, but I still do. Never in my life had I engaged in a light-saber battle before, but apparently I had missed something very great. Sometimes, what I love even more than playing with them is just listening to them play. Hearing their animated voices and intense sound effects as they stage battles around the Bat-cave or fly attacking dragons from secret hidden caves. I have even been known to record these exchanges. They are the sounds of childhood and motherhood, all wrapped into one.

10. Gifts they give me

No matter what I expect to be under the tree waiting for me on request from my husband, I still find myself looking forward to the gifts my children chose for me the most. One Christmas, Caleb exclaimed all morning that he had bought me something sparkly, and I opened a tiny perfume bottle with little fake diamonds haphazardly glued all around the lid. Another year on my birthday, he bought me a silver ring with a turquoise stone, to replace the "old one from Daddy that I always wear," so I could wear one from him instead. Heart. Stopped! And I will never, ever forget the Mother's Day when I opened my gift bag from Toby to find his very own cherished blue rubber ducky inside. "I wanted you to have it, Mommy, because it is *so* special." Yes it is, little boy, yes it is. I still have it.

It's funny now, at the end, to go back over these lists and notice how glaringly the happy stands out above the annoying. And yet—so, *so* many days I can become so completely bogged down by the annoying that the happy almost completely evades me.

When times are hard or when life deals us crushing blows, sometimes my husband and I will quote the question of Job to each other: Shall we take the good from

God, and not the bad? (see Job 2:10). It's a good question. We are eager to gobble up the glorious, but we shy away from the struggles. The two lists in this chapter have me asking the same question, though: Shall we take the good from motherhood, and not the bad? It's a mixed bag, this madness we call motherhood. So much unspeakable beauty. So much teeth-clenching labor (literally). The good and the bad. The petty and the unforgettable. The pain and the pleasure, all rolled into one.

I will take the bad from motherhood, and take it willingly, poop and syrup and all, because I get to take the good as well. The Lord giveth children, and the Lord taketh away sleep. The Lord giveth wonder, and the Lord taketh away flat stomachs. The Lord giveth someone to love, and the Lord taketh away a life only about myself. I'll take it. Blessed be the name of the Lord.

IN CASE YOU GET SIX MINUTES TO YOURSELF: STUDY GUIDE

1. What are some of the things you simply loathe about motherhood?
2. What are some of the blessings you enjoy and cherish about motherhood? (Make a list, if time permits!)
3. Are you more likely to notice the good or the bad in your life right now? Why?
4. Which items on your bad list are stealing your gratitude and joy, and what can you do to change that?
5. Read Job chapters 1 and 2. What messages do these chapters speak into motherhood for you today?
6. Is your relationship with God one that accepts both the good and the bad? If not, why do you have trouble accepting the bad?

Night Cry Psalm

It is long after midnight when I hear the first cry coming from my babies' room. Because their cries are as different as they are, I recognize instantly that it's my little boy twin, Wyatt. I never let my babies cry long for me, if I can help it. So I force myself out of my sleep-warmed bed and walk crookedly down the hall to their room. When I enter and cross to his crib, I can see that he's just waking up—he is hungry and sucking his thumb, but still in that place between sleep and awake, not fully aware. Immediately I scoop him up in my arms and begin to rock him. He soothes peacefully back into sleepy-land.

I guess that's all I wanted from You, God. I wanted You to wrap me in Your arms as soon as sadness or heartbreak and loss came to me. I didn't want You to leave me crying in the dark—but You do God, You do. And You have, so often. Maybe I can't feel Your arms anymore. Maybe my own heart's screams are so loud that they drown out Your voice. I try to make these excuses for You, but they're never good enough. I know—maybe the night is too dark, and You're standing right beside me but I just can't see. Or, maybe you've decided that it's good for me to cry alone.

But that's not who You said You'd be, God. You said You'd never leave me or forsake me. You said You're close to the brokenhearted. What good are arms that hold me close if I can't feel them, God? And of what use is Your presence if my sorrow renders me unable to discern it?

Maybe You are here. Maybe I've become so angry at Your supposed silence that I'm actually choosing not to see You anymore. But wouldn't I still need Your help—even then? Especially then? When do You think people need You the most: when they're peppy and full of faith, or when they're drowning in doubt?

I fear there may be many more hours left of this night I'm living in, Father. Please, please don't leave me here to cry alone. Please show up. Be present, be tangible somehow. Be useful! Be real. I don't need a god in old stories or songs. I don't need a god of theories. I just need arms to hold me while I shatter and sob, until I somehow come to believe that everything in this dark night will soon be OK once again.

IN CASE YOU GET SIX MINUTES TO YOURSELF: STUDY GUIDE

1. When have you felt that God left you alone to cry in darkness? Did He really?
2. What kind of comfort do you expect from God?
3. Read Psalm 130 and Psalm 143. What are three things we can do while we wait on the Lord?
4. What are you waiting on the Lord for today?

Atheist Post

One of my most interesting friends on Facebook is my old buddy Robert the atheist. This might sound odd, but I love to read his posts—particularly the ones denying God, His existence, and His usefulness. Why? Because they challenge, perplex, and fascinate me. I live in a pretty tight Adventist bubble, and sometimes, a peephole through the plastic wrap is actually kind of nice—"Hey—wow! There's a whole world out there!"

Take this post:

> Warning: Atheist Post! I forgot to set my alarm last night but somehow I woke up just in time anyway—not because there is some being prodding me awake, but because my body is programmed to do so. I was able to grab healthy delicious food to take with me before I left the house—not because I have been "blessed," but because my wife and I work hard to earn money to buy it. I got stuck in traffic on the way to work, but happened to find a rare parking spot right outside the front door—not because some imaginary angel saved it for me, but because the guy who occupied it was just pulling out. My car took me to work and back home again because it is made well. I had a wonderful night playing with my children and hanging out with my family, and we didn't need a god in the sky to help us love each other or enjoy each other.

I like to think about his perspective and weigh the validity of his arguments. He's right, on many levels—we can attribute our success to God or choose to attribute it to our own hard work. We can ask for help, but oftentimes no help comes. We can invent "help." And, really, does prayer change the weather? Honestly, I have my doubts . . .

We could debate about these issues for a while. And Christians do—often. But for me, the one question I always come away with after reading Robert's atheist posts is this: What makes us Christians ultimately different from anyone else out there? Because, let's be honest, we all have had those times when we prayed and prayed for something, begged and pleaded with God, and He was silent. He didn't respond, seemingly, or become involved that we could see. Sometimes He does intervene, but if we wanted to doubt, we could say it was just circumstance. Aside from the knowledge that we are somehow "saved," how do Christians actually live differently than atheists?

This year my husband and I were blessed with twin babies—Brooke and Wyatt. Totally unexpected, no pills, twins nowhere in the family. At the same time, Greg received a job transfer out of town. We are unable to move at this time, and so he makes a two-hour commute, staying overnight two to three days a week. Those days and nights without him are so, so terrible. Dinner is eaten in single bites about ten minutes apart. Someone is always crying—always—everything I do is to the background of someone screaming in frantic desperation. Someone is always pooping. Someone is always frantically needing something, and everyone needs me all at once.

The difference is like night and day when Greg comes home—suddenly, there is another set of adult arms! Someone can hold one crying baby while I feed or rock or soothe the other crying one. Someone can help wipe bottoms. Someone can help me clear the table after a meal so that I'm not up doing it at eleven-thirty at night when everyone has finally gone to bed and stayed there. But most important, someone is there to talk to, to listen to my frustrations, to laugh with when I'm covered in some type of bodily slime up to my elbows, and to encourage me when I'm just not sure I'll make it another hour. In those moments when I feel ready to give up, one sympathetic glance from him or one soothing word can give me that extra little push I need to get through. Never before this year have I been more aware of just how important this partnership is to me, to my very emotional stability and survival.

And that, I think, is also one of the (many) things that make Christians different. We still may find ourselves crying a lot of the time. Poop will happen, guaranteed. We will feel overwhelmed, depressed, alone, and at a loss. But Someone will be there. We don't have to navigate this road alone.

I wish that being a Christian also meant none of the bad stuff would happen to us, that we would be protected in a special way, and so on. But it doesn't. What it does mean is companionship for the journey.

Sure, we could make it alone. And many do. It would be harder, but we could make it. But I realized recently that I don't want to. When I could partner with the greatest Friend on earth, why would I choose to go it alone? How grateful I am for that Friend who knows my heart and soul, my weakness and vulnerability, without my ever even having to explain—knows it well enough, even, to teach me something about it.

I have had a lot of faith struggles over the years—if you read my prayer journals, you would see that they are just littered with doubts and questions and discouragement. But no matter what I am questioning or which thing I am struggling with, one thing remains constant on those pages—I thank God for being there. For the fact that I can write to Him, in full and total honesty. Even if I don't get an answer, there is something so necessary to me about the conversation.

I am guessing Robert would argue that he doesn't need this supposed company, because he has enough support in his life already. And maybe I don't "need" it, per se, either. But I want it. And I enjoy it.

IN CASE YOU GET SIX MINUTES TO YOURSELF: STUDY GUIDE

1. When you find yourself asking whether there really is a God or not, what are the things that give you answers, comfort, and faith?
2. Is companionship from God really more desirable than answers and direction? Why? Why not?
3. Do you feel like God is a Companion to you?
4. How would you share the faith and hope that you have with an atheist?
5. What is different about your life because you are a believer?
6. What kind of companionship could you use from God today?

Thirsty

"Mommy, I need a drink! Mommy, I'm *thi-i-i-i-i-i-irsty*!"

There is no way to count how many times a day I hear this simple phrase. I hear it at mealtime—every mealtime—usually half a dozen times (as if the children who were running wild around the house two minutes ago have suddenly forgotten how to walk to the sink). I hear it in the car, about every third stoplight. I hear it breaking through my dreams in the middle of the night, escaping the throat of a child who has walked past three sinks with waiting cups nearby to tell me this. Cries of thirst follow me to every park, every zoo, every store, every doctor's appointment, and every church service I'm pretending I'll actually make it through. Even the children in my house who cannot speak English yet are somehow always telling me they are thirsty. Let me lift a cold glass of water up to my lips and instantly both twins are pointing and frantically screaming, *"Babababababayayayayadiediediemumumumm!"* Or something like that, which I am supposed to automatically translate into "I'm thirsty!" (And I do.) Every child who lives in this house seems to have an insatiable, unquenchable thirst.

Sometimes I just feel the urge to scream at these children, "Can't you see that I'm thirsty too?" Because I am thirsty, desperately thirsty. Not for water (though who among us couldn't use more). Not for juice. Not for milk, or tea, or even coffee. My thirst is the kind that comes from a dry soul and an empty bucket that I still have to keep scraping the bottom of every day. I'm thirsty for energy. Thirsty for more patience. Thirsty for wisdom and love and grace that I can extend to my children. I'm thirsty for meaning and purpose in a life where I spend most of the day doing the same menial chores. I'm thirsty for companionship. I'm thirsty for something that will fill me up so full that I have enough to share with the little people who are constantly needing me to give and give and give. And give some more. I'm thirsty for the type of encounter with God that can carry me through the day.

Ever since I became a mother, I have identified 100 percent with that deer panting for streams of water in Psalm 42. The song is often stuck in my head as a whispered plea, "As the dear panteth for the water, so my soul longeth after Thee." In the original language, we read that the deer isn't looking for just any old water. She's not interested in a trickling, stagnant source, but she is specifically seeking "flowing streams." Something moving, something fresh. Something alive enough to keep her alive too.

That's me. I don't need another stagnant story or a slow seeping of life—no. I need something fresh, flowing, alive, and new, and I need it fast.

There are quite a few places in the Bible where Jesus takes care of people's thirst or hunger. The wedding at Cana, the feeding of the five thousand by the sea. I have noticed in most of these stories that while we see Jesus asking for food or water, He hardly ever does it solely for Himself. When He met the woman at the well in John 4 and asked for a drink of water, what He actually did instead was quench the heart-thirst of a girl five times rejected and forgotten. When He asks for the boy's lunch of loaves and fishes, it is to feed others. When He sends servants to fill up jars of water at the wedding, they come back sweet enough to please even the most critical of guests. We know that He ate and drank with sinners, but in every case recorded, it was the sinners who came away heart-quenched. Even at the Last Supper, He had requested bread and juice to be set up in order that the disciples may have a lasting "remembrance" of His sacrifice. Jesus' thirst, His act of drinking in the Scriptures, always seems to be centered around serving other people.

Until the cross.

As He hangs there bleeding and dying, we finally hear Him make a request for Himself, and Himself only: "I am thirsty." The Man who could create food and drink from almost nothing found Himself without. The Man who offered the water of life that could quench a thirst forever was thirsty. The mouth that commands all water— He who spoke the seas into existence and tells the clouds when to rain and orders the storms to stop—this mouth is dry. He is thirsty. And this thirst goes completely unquenched. I think that my Lord died thirsty.

But He died thirsty so that I don't have to live thirsty. All of the things my soul yearns for every day can be found in Him. All of the needs that pile up in my life can be met in Him. Every desire, every empty place in my soul can be filled. His is the well that never runs dry.

So when I do end up parched and thirsty in my life, I guess it's usually because I haven't visited the well. Or because I've been trying to satisfy my thirst at other places and in other ways. Whenever I sit down at the well that is Jesus Christ and take a long refreshing drink—or even just a hurried sip—I am filled in a way that nothing else on earth can quite compare to.

It's a thirsty time of life, these early motherhood years. I get pretty desperate and dry. So many people depend on me for so very much, every day. I have to keep giving even when I'm sick, exhausted, lifeless, raging, brokenhearted, or hopeless. And because that is exactly as impossible as it sounds, I know my source needs to be found somewhere other than myself. For some reason, I take comfort in the knowledge that the only One who can fill my thirst also truly knew thirst Himself. That works for me. O God who hung far lower than the frayed end of my rope—find and fill my weary, thirsting soul today.

IN CASE YOU GET SIX MINUTES TO YOURSELF: STUDY GUIDE

1. Do you identify with the idea of being soul thirsty right now?
2. Why does something as rewarding as motherhood still have the ability to empty you so much?
3. What methods have you used to fill yourself? Which work, and which fail? Why?
4. Read Psalm 42. What answers does this psalm give in times of thirst?
5. Read the story of the woman at the well in John 4. In what ways is her story similar to your own right now?
6. Contemplate Jesus thirsty on the cross. What does that scene teach you about His knowledge of your humanity and limitations?
7. What is it exactly that you are thirsting most deeply for today?

Sacred Places

I used to travel the world—once upon a time—but now as a young mother with babies and toddlers and debt up to my earlobes, I think it's time to admit those days are over. Those days, in fact, have come to a sickening, screeching halt. It's almost impossible, presently, to even imagine a time when someone won't need me for their basic survival or when the top-ten list of lenders I owe money to will be paid off and crossed off forever. Right about the time they are, I'll be staring college bills dead in the face anyway. So I finally just had to make peace with the fact that, sadly, my traveling days are likely over. I gave up that life when I became a mother. But . . . I *used* to travel the world. It still feels great to say that.

During my travels across various continents and countries, the places that always seem to flash brightest in my memories are the "sacred places." I have watched the sun rise from the highest pinnacle of Mount Sinai, gripping the red, craggy rocks against the wind as the first orange rays spilled across the desolate Sinai desert, and there I pondered Moses receiving the commandments in fire and earthquakes. I have knelt beside Aztec altars where infants and virgins were sacrificed to appease angry gods, and I have run my shaking hands over the white, sun-bleached rocks where they died. There was a time when I crept through a crowded Roman youth hostel and shook my groggy husband awake before dawn to catch a train so that we could be the first lone visitors to enter Saint Peter's Basilica in absolute silence. From deep within the bowels of the ancient great pyramids, I raised my voice in spontaneous hymns that echoed off the thousands-of-years-old stones of a false burial chamber. I remember the hot Peruvian wind on my neck as I knelt in prayer at Machu Picchu. I still feel the dried banana leaves tickling my sandaled feet in the ruins of an ancient Tahitian temple surrounded by sugar cane stalks. And I could have wandered for hours upon hours through the blush-red mazes of the endless Japanese torii-gate tunnels at the Fushimi Inari shrine, which is known for calling travelers to seek, pray, and journey. Sacred places.

A place becomes sacred for various reasons—its history, human tradition, the commemoration of events that took place upon its grounds, and similar such things. Every culture and, in fact, every religion have their own set of sacred places, and these are always the "must see" recommendations in any guidebook worth its salt. So we visit them, we exist in their spaces for a moment, and we try to connect with the people and the times and the gods that made them sacred.

I always have thought that I could have handpicked these places without the guidebook or cab driver's advice because the sacred is something palpable—something you can feel. The wadded up prayer papers shoved desperately through crevices in the rock wall surrounding the alleged "burning bush" of Moses, the unmistakable sound of the singing bells of Westminster Abbey—you can feel those things. Nobody forgets the feeling of that first startled glimpse of the treasury through the narrow red-walled canyons of Petra, though everybody tries to describe it. I sometimes wish to forget the echoes of shame reverberating off the pile of shoes in the Holocaust Museum, the charred remains of a girl's lunch encased in glass to commemorate the Hiroshima bombing, or the open floor of the commanding Coliseum revealing the maze of tunnels where the captives were held until they were summoned to fight to their deaths.

"I'm so sorry," we whisper in horror. Our hearts instinctively know these places to be sacred.

Other sacred places that I've visited cannot be found on any maps or in any guide books, but I recognized them as being sacred just as easily. I believe we can sense the presence or the memory of something holy. Nobody marked the rain reflecting off the single-file line of Japanese lanterns glowing through the deserted streets in Kyoto, but my soul remembers the tranquility of that night. I was the only person who heard the untranslatable evening song of the little Marshallese boy collecting shells for the strange blond girl crying on the rocks, but I knew the place was sacred as soon as he gingerly placed the first shell in my hand. Something happens to us in these places. Our pace slows. We fall into a marked quiet. We open our eyes and ears and tune in to our surroundings. We feel connected to a Higher Presence. And we leave just a tad bit different than we came—touched, humbled, inspired. The sacred places work their magic on us in the same ways I imagine they did for people hundreds and thousands of years ago, who came before us.

I honestly don't have many acquaintances who could make a list of sacred places that competes with mine. Only a small sampling of my friends can say they've imagined the baptism of Jesus as they gazed on the muddy waters of the Jordan before them, walked where He likely walked near the Sea of Galilee, or stooped to collect pottery shards in the dust of the ruins of the Decapolis. How many people, when they drink hot mint tea, are instantly transported back to a Bedouin tent in Jordan's red valleys, still able to hear the haunting foreign laments they sang as they passed around the steaming cups? Lots of travelers build cairns on their journeys to mark that they have been by, but probably for the rest of my life, whenever I see the rock cairns of travelers, I will remember balancing the rocks of my own cairn near Elijah's spring in the hot afternoon Egyptian sun. I'm proud of my list. I mourned my list when I realized I wouldn't be expanding it anymore, because I knew that nothing in stay-at-home motherhood life could ever compare to the wonders I've seen and experienced.

But that was before the rug.

Beside my son's little toddler bed lies a small, square giraffe-and-elephant rug. My mother-in-law ordered this rug online for me when I was pregnant, to match the jungle décor theme I had chosen for the room. When it came in the mail, I thought it was cute, sure, but never would have guessed it to be anything more. However, this unlikely little rug has somehow slowly become a sacred place to me, over the four short years of my son's life. And it is so sacred, in fact, that I might even go so far as to call it more sacred than all of the other places I listed above combined.

I can often be found here in the middle of the night, on my knees on this childish rug, hunched over my boy's sleeping frame. It is here that I plead with the Lord to stand in the gap of all my mistakes and shortcomings and flat-out failures as a mother. I beg for wisdom and forgiveness and patience. This rug waits patiently as I pour out my soul to God, explaining how lost I feel, and how inept at motherhood I truly am. It catches my tears when I stroke his cherub cheeks and beg his sleeping face for forgiveness of the yelling, the snapping, the angry outburst, and the preoccupied ignoring that transpired that day. "I'm so sorry," I whisper in horror.

The rug expects me to question what darkness lies inside me that would cause me to treat my own child so carelessly. It absorbs all of my insecurity and self-hatred, yet still permits me to kiss him, brush the hair off his forehead. And each time, the rug knowingly allows me to end by once again purposing in my heart to change my ways and be the very best mother any child has ever had anywhere. "I'll do better," I promise him in the dark—him, and myself. And the rug pretends to believe. It's not a magic rug—it doesn't infuse me with selfless love or erase my many faults, to be sure; otherwise I wouldn't have to keep coming back. It's just an understanding rug. It knows why I've come. It is willing to hold me in my regret.

What makes this place sacred, I have come to understand, is the same thing that makes all the others sacred too: what happens there. I meet God in the quiet. I take an honest look square in the face at the ugliest sides of myself. I reflect on a path hundreds have trod before me. I remember what matters most. I ponder the reason I was put on this earth. Something significant shifts inside of me. And I determine that I will not leave here the same.

Please be assured that—of course—I have had significant times of prayer in many other far more exotic places. I once walked through the pink sand of a Bermuda beach and implored God to somehow help my struggling marriage survive. And He did. From the third floor of a worn-down Marshall Islands mission school building on the island of Ebeye, I sought God in a panic to help me somehow teach His love to students who barely spoke English. He did that too. Suspended in a rope hammock under palms and stars in the Jamaican night sky, the very month before my first son made his arrival into our lives, my husband and I prayed that God would find a way to make us good parents. That prayer hasn't finished yet, but it's why I come to the rug. And looking back now, I consider the rug to be just as sacred and just as enticing as the Jamaican beach. There aren't any teal blue waters, but there's hope, and I crave that more.

I've still never seen the pillars of the Parthenon, and I'd really like to walk the Via Dolorosa through Jerusalem before I die. Perhaps even tread the haunted grounds of Auschwitz. Stand on the island of Patmos. Tour the Taj Mahal. Keep pace with lions in a Kenyan safari jeep. But even if I never get the chance to visit one more sacred place for the rest of my life, I think I could be content with just the giraffe-and-elephant rug. I could. And the reason for that is simple: I'm not after conquests and bucket lists and travel tallies anymore. I'm after the eternal soul of my son and the tools with which to shape his character for a lifetime. Those tools can't be found on the banks of the Seine under Notre Dame's shadow or nestled under coral at the bottom of the Red Sea—though I've navigated both those waters once. Those tools can only be found in harder waters to navigate—in earnest petition to my heavenly Father. And I guess that the petition of an earnest heart really can take place anywhere on earth, and for that reason any place can become sacred when we contact God from it.

I think of young Jacob on the run, ghosts of Esau and his death threats dancing in his head as he passes out on his stone pillow. The dream, the ladder, the angels. An unforgettable promise, and an undeniable meeting with God. When Jacob awakes, he can feel it on his skin just as we all can: this is a sacred place. In fact he even names the place Bethel, which means "house of God," and says, "Surely the LORD is in this place, and I was not aware of it" (Genesis 28:16). But he is aware now. God met him there, in his sacred place, and he will never be the same again. The house of God is not a place, it is every place—it is wherever He chooses to meet us—be it an ancient pyramid, a stone pillow, or a child's rug. Actually, there is no place on earth where He *can't* meet us, and this comforts me greatly. I love this story, because I am in need of a God who can find me instead of a God that I will somehow have to find.

I don't know where you've traveled, and I don't know whether you have one cherished traveling memory or many. Maybe you, too, have laid down a lot for your child and changed your life significantly in the process. But whoever you are, wherever you've been, and whatever you've done, I hope you find a sacred place. I hope you protect a point in space and time where you can come to God simply as yourself. As a traveler. As someone on a journey, asking for directions, seeking a destination. And I hope that, even if you have to stop traveling the world for logistical reasons, that you never stop traveling with God, because there is no reason and nothing that should stop you. No—not even the mistakes you've made. In fact, any good traveler knows that one day your mistakes will make the best-celebrated stories.

The time will probably come when my son is awakened by my weary self-loathing Mommy frame leaning over him in the dead of night. I hope he's not afraid. At minimum, he will want an explanation. I'm not sure what I will tell him on that night, except that this is my sacred place. I hope that he will somehow find a way to understand. Maybe he won't understand until he has a sacred place of his own, at the foot of his own son's bed, where he pleads to be better than he is. I hope he will call me on that night, if he does finally understand. To be perfectly honest, I hope he has to make a long-distance call to India somewhere outside the Taj Mahal. But chances are more likely that he'll find me in the simplicity of my own small bedroom. And if it's the middle of the night, and if my foolish and nostalgic imagination could have its way, his call would catch me kneeling on a faded and torn giraffe-and-elephant rug, moved to my room years before. I hope it finds me still there on my knees, praying for him.

IN CASE YOU GET SIX MINUTES TO YOURSELF: STUDY GUIDE

1. Where are some of the sacred places you have traveled to or visited?
2. Where are your own personal sacred places—places where God has met you?
3. One of the themes in this chapter is what we have given up for our children, and we often stop the tallies there. But what have you gained from having your children that life without them never could have brought you?
4. Another theme is the guilt and regret, even sometimes perfectionistic striving, that we experience as mothers. Can and should these types of feelings be avoided? Why?
5. Read the story of Jacob's sacred place in Genesis 28. Why was God's particular promise so significant at that time in Jacob's life?
6. How are you doing at protecting the sacred places and spaces in your daily walk with God? How could your experience of motherhood benefit from more time in sacred spaces?
7. If God were to meet you today with a promise for your future, what would you desire it to be?

Midnight Meltdown

The clock reads 2:26 A.M. when I finally step out of the little room where my babies sleep. In truth, I'm not altogether sure what just happened here . . .

My five-month-old baby boy must have been sick or in pain or something else, because his normally sweet, easy-going disposition was temporarily replaced by a snarling, raging monster who refused to be comforted in any way. And I tried—I tried everything, believe me. For hours.

Instead of snuggling into my arms as he usually does when I rock him to sleep, tonight he kicked and screamed and flailed. I turned him around so he could rest his head on my shoulder as I patted his back—he loves this normally—but tonight it made him screech and holler as though he was being tortured. He beat his chubby fists against my head and repeatedly arched his back to push away from me with all the strength his little body could muster.

Next we tried "walking"—that aimless wandering and pacing throughout the house that sleep-deprived parents know all too well. This actually worked.

For two blessed minutes.

The cruel tease of false victory was cut short by a sudden outburst of wailing and weeping. His little fists clawed desperately at my hair, pulling and yanking so hard that I wanted to wail myself. I was able to successfully untangle one hand of miniature vise-grip fingers from my hair. But when I went after the second hand, the first hand began grasping at my ear, twisting and scraping the inside folds with razor-sharp corners of jagged infant fingernails. I did scream in shock that time—*"Ouch!"* I yelled—to the night, to no one. In response to my scream, his cries turned to guttural growls—the angriest noises he can make. He began coughing and sputtering for air in between, all the while continuing to fight me.

In the midst of all this fury and rage, an epiphany came to me: Maybe he did not want to be held. Was I overstimulating him? Did he simply want to be left alone to suck his thumb to sleep, as he often does? With his shrill infant voice ringing in my bleeding ear, I carried him back to his room and curled him into bed on his side—just how he likes. Instantly, he found his thumb and began sucking it, with his other hand over his eyes—the classic sleep position.

I congratulated myself on knowing my baby well and breathed a sigh of relief that the madness was over. My shoulders relaxed, my pulse slowed. Sweet sleep would soon be mine, and I was oh-so-ready after this battle. Backing up a few feet out of his sight, I waited a moment, just to be sure he was truly OK.

He was truly not OK. After less than a minute, he began flailing, kicking, and sobbing. *Again.* But this time he was downright frantic. His red puffy eyes began searching all around his crib in every direction, and I realized then that he was looking for me. Though I was only a few feet away, he could not see me. His panic intensified. Certain I had left him alone and abandoned, he screamed for me desperately, with a sound that reminded me of a cat fight I had recently woken up to in the night.

He was red-faced and his entire body was trembling by the time I scooped him up. I wrapped him in my arms and shushed into his little ears, where tears had pooled and were overflowing down his neck. His whole body instantly relaxed in relief and exhaustion. His crying subsided into tiny gasps and sighs, and I rocked him and sang to him as he calmed down. "Mommy's here," I whispered. "Mommy loves you." His head grew gradually heavier against my chest. I could tell that he was on his way to sleep at long last.

Until the explosion came. I felt it, heard it, and smelled it all together in one awful realization. So did he. What should have registered as relief set him instead to bitter screams of rage. I shook my head, amused that someone could be so offended by their own bodily functions. I didn't notice the warm sensation until we were halfway to the changing table. But one quick look confirmed my fears—the poop explosion had shot out the diaper, up his back, through his pajamas, and onto the front of my T-shirt. Telltale yellowish-green stains were quickly creeping across us both.

For some reason, this sent me over the edge. All along I had been worried, anxious, concerned for my baby, but now I was just royally ticked off. I was seriously in jeopardy of "losing my Christianity," as my husband calls it. You know—those instances when you picture only for a split second how satisfying it would be to just throw in the towel. (See, you're not the only one who's ever had those thoughts!) These are the moments when we parents digress into the dangerous dens of why-mes and what-ifs and how-much-longers. I actually think the mundane tasks of cleaning and care manage to save us in these times, anchor us back to the earth in some sort of quiet resignation.

Slowly I changed him first, layer by sticky layer, before changing my own soiled shirt. And then I settled down yet again to nurse him to sleep. The awful escapade just had to be almost over, I told myself. Soon he would be fast asleep in my arms. This time, I was right. He fell asleep. But only after a choking fit which ended in sour milk throw-up all over my freshly changed shirt. At this, he finally seemed satisfied, and having wreaked all the havoc he could manage to in one night, he happily drifted off to sleep with a smile.

What happened next was maybe even harder to predict than all the rest. Instead of dragging out of the room in relief, a strange desire came over me to just stay and continue to hold him. So I did. I sat there for a long time, throw-up drying on my clothes, staring at the beautiful features of his relaxed little face. The weight of his small body grew heavier by the minute, but for some reason I could not put down this sleeping child. I was mesmerized, the way only the truly sleep-deprived and adrenaline-crashed can be. I smiled at his fluttering eyelids. I traced circles around his little cheeks, nuzzled the tip of his pug nose with my own, and kissed his slightly open triangle mouth again and again. I listened to his rhythmic breathing and petted the thin hair on his mostly bald little head. My heart spontaneously welled up with love beyond measure for this precious bundle. When I gingerly picked up his hand to hold it, I noticed pieces of my own hair still clenched tightly in a balled fist—the last remnants of the night's battle.

As I sat there rocking him, loving him, and enjoying him in the gift of those last surprising moments, an old familiar Bible text somehow threaded its way into my memory. Something, perhaps, from the book of Isaiah? I couldn't remember the numbers, but the words snuck up on me in perfect order: "As a mother comforts her child, so will I comfort you" (Isaiah 66:13).

I literally stifled a laugh.

Before I was a mother, I used to read this verse and conjure up the idea of a lovely maternal woman serenely rocking a sweet, cooing baby to sleep in her poised arms. The baby smiled adoringly up at her, in my vision, as she caressed his tiny cheeks and beamed back in joy—the perfect picture of nurture, peace, and comfort.

Then I had my own children.

And I learned that real mommy comfort usually looks a whole lot more like this night I've just endured. A mother is an amazing creature, if I may say so myself. She will continue to comfort her child even through the most piercing screams and the most painful bouts of scratching, punching, or kicking. We mamas can be hit, bit, pooped on, and covered in barf, but there is something in us that will continue to offer comfort, yes—even in the midst of our own pain and frustration.

It put a smile on my face that night to realize that *this*—this is how my God comforts me. Not with quiet soothing in a rocking chair, not with gentle pats from His faraway cloud in the sky, but with His sleeves rolled up in the filth and the grime of my real-life messes. He's not repulsed by the ugliest things I throw His way—my habits, my secrets, my shame. He's also not afraid of my fury. He comforts me when I'm screaming in anger in His face—and I have done this more times than I care to admit. He holds me when I'm raging and wild with hate. He accepts the reality of my own fists clenched around the things I cannot seem to let go of—destructive things I choose above Him. He endures any attempts my jagged edges might make to bloody

His name (or His body, as history has shown), but He never loses His patience as we do. Though I may throw elaborate grown-up tantrums, He isn't tempted to throw me down the stairs.

If He must step aside when I insist on pushing Him away, He's never too far off. I may feel abandoned, ignored, or even left for dead. I may question His goodness, seethe at His silence, or fling accusations that He doesn't care, that He isn't there. But He waits in love nearby, close enough to scoop my doubting self right back up into His arms again, just as soon as I say the word. And when those rare moments come (Do they come?) when I happen to be easy, obedient, and good, He's not relieved to put me aside and move on to something else. Instead, I believe He holds me, cherishes me, enjoys the company of a child whom He loves beyond measure.

Frankly, I like this picture of God so much better than the perfect one. I like it that He's big enough to handle all my anger, all my ugliness, and all my failings. He's big enough to handle me. This gives me permission to be real with Him—to be the realest, most despicable version of me—because His arms can take it. As a mother comforts her child, so He will comfort me—through the deepest storm, through the darkest night, at any cost to Himself—He will comfort me.

The clock reads 2:26 A.M. when I finally step out of the little room where my babies sleep. But instead of leaving in discouragement and defeat, I leave comforted.

IN CASE YOU GET SIX MINUTES TO YOURSELF: STUDY GUIDE

1. What is the most epic meltdown you have endured with your children thus far in motherhood?
2. What is the most epic meltdown you have waged against God in your own anger and fury and frustration?
3. What kind of parent do you picture God to be?
4. Think of the worst sides of yourself. Do you believe God is big enough to handle even that? Have you taken it to Him recently?
5. Read Isaiah 66. How is the picture of God as a comforting parent significant to you today?
6. Where in your life do you need the most comfort right now?

Pajama Day

He declared the day "pajama day"—one full day in which the entire family would not change out of our pajamas or leave the house for any reason. I thought Caleb would want to visit zoos and children's museums and parks, and have grand adventures during his spring break. So I planned these things. But he had other ideas—a whole day just at home together. "I have to get up every single day, Mommy, and get dressed and go out," he explained. "So I just want one day that I can stay in my jammies and don't have to go anywhere!" Since pajama day was what he wanted, pajama day is what took place on that gray Wednesday in March: nobody got dressed, and we all stayed home.

At first, I was disappointed and, I admit, a little frantic about it. I'm not a student anymore, but as a mother, I look forward to spring break too—all those days with my son here with me instead of at school where I'm missing him. I wanted to make lots of family memories and have special bonding time. I had planned a trip to Mount Baker to play in the snow that Wednesday, and already I found myself imagining the great photos I would take and the fun Facebook updates I would post. In comparison, a whole day at home didn't sound exciting at all. In fact, that's kind of what I do every day already—wander around in my pajamas until afternoon, trapped in the house, doing chores.

Somehow, this day turned out differently though. I put on Pandora after breakfast, and when Disney's *Frozen* soundtrack came up we belted out "Let It Go!" together at the top of our lungs as we danced around the living room. This resulted in a game of magically freezing each other (and the cat) and building imaginary ice castles out of blanket forts. Which naturally led to Superman role-playing in his polar ice castle, and of course Jedi Knights sprang into action to help Superman. The day progressed in the laughter of little-boy superhero daydreams. I found myself listening around corners and stifling giggles at their bizarre imaginary scenarios and their intense light-saber battles for freedom of the galaxy.

Back upstairs by myself, I poured a cup of jasmine tea, lit some candles, and spontaneously scooped up my baby boy for a dance to "Somewhere Over the Rainbow." I wrote in my journal and unpacked boxes waiting since the last Christmas. Sitting on the kitchen floor with my twins, I had sticky fingers gleefully pressing too many tangerine quarters into my mouth. I curled up in my husband's lap at his desk and shared a ministry idea for our church that came to me in the hallway. Late in the day, we swam in the hot tub together—all six of us. When it got dark, we gathered beside a backyard fire pit, sang songs, and told stories into the night. It was by far the best day of the entire spring break—even the zoo trips and beach hikes and snow adventures (which I forced back into the week) couldn't compare.

Sometime during the afternoon of pajama day, I caught myself staring out at the potted yellow pansies on the deck swaying against the gray sky and perceived one profound thought with distinct clarity: I felt full to the brim with happiness and contentment. Those two elusive friends I find myself hunting for in vain on too many days, yet here they appeared on their own. *What made the difference?* I wondered later. Just another day at home, like so many others. Was it the absence of a schedule? A day unhindered by previous plans? Giving myself permission for playful moments? The freedom from expectations, perhaps? I'm really not quite sure. I just know that something happened here, on pajama day, something extraordinary. For the first time in many weeks, we experienced a "Sabbath" of sorts.

My family has always observed a Sabbath rest once a week—one day off in seven when we do no work. From sundown Friday to sundown Saturday (and often beyond), we worship, we recharge, we enjoy nature, we reconnect in relationships, and we spend time together. I love Sabbath, and I always have. Here's what I love: I love the freedom to look at a sink full of dishes and just walk away, instead telling myself, "Not today. Work can wait." The license to play with my children on the floor instead of feeling a compulsion to pick up the toys around us. The liberty of closing the laundry-room door for a full, blessed twenty-four hours. The indulgence of quiet hours for Bible study, journaling, reading, and searching once the children go to bed at night. The unmistakable feeling that I have been with Jesus. Exemption from the rat race, and the God-given right to just stop. Exist. Enjoy. Rest. Be free.

Why did God put these pajama-day Sabbaths into every week and then ask us to observe them (Exodus 20:8–11)? Because I think He knew that we would seriously *need* them. It's too easy to spin endlessly on the hamster wheel, buried under our schedules, trapped in the frenetic need to find our value in what we produce and contribute to society. Stepping out of this madness for one day, once a week, reminds us that the world doesn't own us—God does. We remember whose image we are shaped in, and we give ourselves the chance to enjoy the liberation of God's love.

Some rabbis teach that those who observe the Sabbath become able to keep all the other commandments as well. Why is this? Because on Sabbath we practice telling ourselves no. And when we practice denying ourselves in one area, we not only become quite accomplished at it, but we also suddenly become able to say no in other areas too. Following this line of logic, if there's a struggle or sin in our life that we can't seem to master, we ought to try keeping the Sabbath regularly. Saying no to work and the world on one day boosts our self-control enough to say no to temptations on all days.

The thing is, I could make many more long lists about why I keep the Sabbath, and I could compile compelling Scripture texts to support my certainty that the day matters and has never changed.* But what's most convincing to me, beyond any proof-text list or reason rundown, is the satisfying *experience* of simply enjoying it. I am a different woman at the end of the Sabbath—less hurried, more centered, more free. We are a different family, we are more connected, and the unmistakable presence of Jesus is marked among us. All arguments aside—who doesn't want those things? I know I do. I need Sabbaths and pajama days because I start to forget what real life is all about. I get cold, and I need to return to the warmth of God's fires.

"How is your own deep fire doing, by the way? Are you pretty confident that you have enough heat and warmth and light within yourself to get you through the night?"† If your schedule-ridden soul is getting worn out and burned out from the constant wear and tear of the machine that is life, schedule yourself a pajama day. Find a Sabbath. Rediscover your purpose, reconnect with your family, and recommit to your God. You are many things to many people, but above all of these, you are a daughter of the King.

IN CASE YOU GET SIX MINUTES TO YOURSELF: STUDY GUIDE

1. When was the last time your family celebrated a sort of pajama day or a day off like the one described above?
2. What was the cause of the unexpected joy in the author's pajama day? Do you regularly find those pockets of joy and contentment in your own life? If not, what could be the reason why?

---

* Jesus didn't expect the day to change after His death or He wouldn't have told the disciples in Matthew 24 to pray that their flight from Jerusalem didn't take place on the Sabbath. Why say this if He didn't expect them to continue keeping it? The Bible teaches that once God has blessed something, it is blessed forever and man cannot change it (see Numbers 23:19, 20; 1 Chronicles 17:26, 27; Ecclesiastes 3:14; Genesis 2:2, 3). The Sabbath was not "done away with" in the Mosaic law because the Sabbath was given far before the law—at Creation (Genesis 2:2, 3). Jesus didn't participate in the silly traditions of man, but He *did* keep the Sabbath (Luke 4:16; Matthew 5:17). The apostles kept the Sabbath long after Jesus left (Acts 17:2; 18:4; 13:14, 42, 43; 16:13). Keeping God's commandments will be a trademark of God's true people at the end of time (Revelation 12:17; 14:12). God even states that we will be keeping the Sabbath throughout eternity in the new earth (Isaiah 66:22, 23).

† Barbara Brown Taylor, *An Altar in the World* (New York: HarperCollins, 2009), 136.

3. What are/could be the benefits of keeping the Sabbath? What are the challenges? Which outweighs the other?

4. Read the arguments in the first footnote on page 70 and look up the verses listed. Which of these is the most convincing reason to *you* for keeping the Sabbath?

5. Make two lists: one list of all the things you have to get done, and another list of all the things you *want* to do. Put the lists where you can see them often. Which list does your heart scream for? What does that tell you?

6. If you took one twenty-four-hour period weekly just to spend with God and family, how might your life be different?

7. Where are the broken places inside you that could use a Sabbath rest to heal?

Children's Hospital

t is a place you never want to imagine checking your own child into. But here she is, twisting in my arms at the registration desk in her pink polka-dot mouse pajamas that I lifted her out of bed in. Why does she belong here, among these sick kids—isn't she perfect and happy and well? No; the answer resounds in hollow reality—no, she is not. That's why we're here.

We wait in the lobby—my husband Greg, Brooke, and I—where they will soon call her name for surgery. She pat-pat-pats the aquarium glass as a large tropical blue tang swims by. "Fee-fee!" she exclaims in delight, followed by more glass patting. "Yes, big fishy!" I agree. Oh, she is so darling, so unspeakably precious to me, this little girl I call "Missy Tiny." I cannot help it—I know this is awful—but just for a moment I entertain the fear that these could be our last moments with her. *Please God,* I silently beg, *please let this surgery go OK. Please help her to be just fine.* The doctors have assured us the surgery is safe—but don't things happen sometimes? I look around at the solemn stares of the other parents in the surgery center lobby and wonder exactly how many silent prayers are being lifted here today, how many are lifted here *every* day.

There is death on every face here. On some it is very prominent—the bald heads of cancer, for example. On others it looks more ghostly—the news freshly received, the stumbling in disbelief for the doorway. Some carry with them the death of hopes: all the dreams they had planned for their children that can no longer come to pass. But even amongst those without dying children, there are deaths. Some are mourning the death of faith: "God, how could You let this happen to us? If You loved us, if You existed, this wouldn't be." Others are mourning the death of normalcy: no one is immune from tragedy, and life will never be the same again. We face the death of security in those rooms—we no longer believe that nothing bad could ever happen to *our* little family, because it has. The death of ignorance, that there are families out there suffering in these rooms daily while we go about our business, mowing lawns and washing the car. The death of ungratefulness: we will not, cannot, leave these halls without clutching our children tightly and breathing silent thanks for the horrors we have been spared from—if we are spared. We will no longer take small moments for granted, we promise ourselves, because we realize with painful clarity that nobody is guaranteed an endless supply of them.

"Brooke Howell?" A male nurse in green scrubs calls her name, and this is our moment. We follow him back, she is fitted into the tiniest hospital gown I have ever seen, and we wait. Finally, I am allowed to accompany her into the operating room, where a little mask full of strawberry-flavored anesthetic air covers her face, and she drifts peacefully off to sleep.

"OK! She did well. We'll page you when she's finished, Mom!" they assure me good-naturedly. They are so confident, but surely they must say this all day. Do all the mothers look as awful as I feel? I wander down the maze of hospital hallways and corridors, back to the lobby, and when the blue tang swims by, I feel a very sharp pang in my heart, because there are no small hands there to pat-pat-pat him. There is nothing to do now but wait. Greg tries to read a magazine, but I know it's not working because he never turns the page. Minutes pass, or hours—I can't really tell which. I hang on to every round the blue tang makes around the tank. I think of the words David wrote in the Psalms, somewhere: "My soul waits for the LORD more than watchmen [wait] for the morning, more than watchmen [wait] for the morning" (130:6, RSV). *I am the watchman on the city walls today, Father, and I am waiting for You with every breath, waiting for You to show up, waiting for the news that You have done what I've begged You to do. Waiting for those first rays of hope's sun.*

My mind wanders, thankfully, to something else—still related—the phone call from a good friend yesterday evening, who called to say she'd be praying for us here today. "Thank you," I said, "that means a lot to me. I'm scared for her."

"Why?" The friend's tone suddenly changed. "Why are you scared? Don't you trust that God will take care of her? You know that everything's going to be fine. God will heal her. Where's your faith, Melissa?"

The words set my blood's temperature to instant boil, and I could feel the righteous indignation coursing through my veins.

"My faith is right here, actually," I defended myself. "And I believe God can heal her—completely. But my faith also allows for God to be God. If He chooses not to heal her, for whatever reason, my faith has to survive that too."

"Well I hope she's OK," chided my friend, "when you say things like that. I think you should just trust Him, Melissa."

"But I do trust Him!" I insisted. "I trust Him with either outcome, don't you see? Don't you realize that God never promises to answer all of our prayers? That bad things happen to good, faithful, praying families every day? What, do you think that all the kids who will be wheeled into chemotherapy rooms tomorrow have parents who didn't have enough faith?" I was angry. As I think about it now, I'm still angry.

The blue tang is swimming faster, darting side to side, and I think he's angry too.

"Well, I don't know about that, but we know that God works all things together for *good*," my false-encourager emphasized. "In any case, *I* will be praying that she is completely healed."

I review this conversation in my head, over and over again. Is this what all theologians do in hospital waiting rooms—look for sinkholes in their theology? Will our theology save our children? Not necessarily. But it might save us through whatever happens. The more I think about the phone call, the more solidified in my own position I become. My mind turns (thankfully—another distraction) to the three Hebrews, head and shoulders above everyone else in the crowd that is bowing down to the golden statue. I remember their chilling words: "If we are thrown into the blazing furnace, the God we serve is able to deliver us from it, and he will deliver us from Your Majesty's hand. *But even if he does not,* we want you to know, Your Majesty, that we will not serve your gods or worship the image of gold you have set up" (Daniel 3:17, 18; emphasis added).

This assurance of God's ability, coupled with an allowance for His sovereignty—this is what I'm hanging my theological hat on today. It's far safer, for the endurance of my own faith, to trust God with *any* outcome than to expect Him to answer every prayer exactly the way I want Him to. We must accept the "even if He doesn't" times. God never promised to spare us from every tragedy, did He? On the contrary, most of the Bible heroes suffered greatly for their faith, and God allowed it, for whatever reason. So I don't think true faith expects a "Yes" answer every time—that's not faith, that's presumption. True faith, rather, is the firm commitment to serve God no matter what, regardless of the outcome. "Shall we accept the good from God, and not the bad?" Job asked, and the answer seems obvious.

Do I have this faith? I wonder, as the blue tang eyes me. *When the doctors tell us whatever they're going to tell us in a few minutes, is my faith ready to hear anything? To accept all outcomes? My soul waits for the Lord more than watchmen wait for the morning, more than watchmen wait for the morning.* I'm pacing those city walls again, waiting for the sun.

Once I was told by a friend from seminary that people in Africa pray extremely differently from those of us in America. We beg and plead with God to take our suffering away, to spare us from heartache and shield us from horrors. But Africans must know better. They must understand that these bad things are largely unavoidable, that they are, in fact, just a part of life. So instead of asking God to intervene and take their suffering away, they simply pray for the strength to endure it. The courage to get through it and to bear it well. In my mind, that kind of prayer can be summed up in one word: acceptance. "The LORD gave, and the LORD hath taken away; blessed be the name of the LORD" (Job 1:21, KJV).

I am no Job, I realize, in the stuffy waiting room. I am too scared.

The pager vibrates in my lap, and Greg and I both rush to the desk eagerly. "She's out of surgery and doing well," the nurse assures us at the front, "but the surgeon is going to come and talk with you for a few minutes. So please sit here; he'll be just a minute." We are ushered into a smaller room, one with a closed door and no windows. What kind of a room is this? What kind of news gets dropped on people in here? And where is the fish that I need right now? The nurse must have read the horror on my face, because he said, "Don't worry, we do this for every family—everyone gets to chat with the surgeon about how the procedure went." I feel better, but not really.

Within a few minutes, the surgeon is sitting down with us, and he's smiling—oh, I could hug him; surely there can't be bad news if he's smiling! "Well," he begins, "she did great. She's waking up now." And I am instantly crying. *Oh, God. Thank You, thank You, God.* "But there is definitely more in there than we expected," he explains. We are shown pictures—MRI images—of tumors, so many tumors. A tumor system that twists and turns with no bounds and seems to fill up the entire cavity of her abdomen. Tumors wound around her kidneys, past her liver, tumors everywhere. I can't explain what it's like to see this and grasp the fact that it lives inside your very own child. There are no words. "These are lymphatic abnormalities," the kind surgeon explains, "and they are *not* cancerous," he emphasizes. We take the breath that I didn't realize we'd been holding. "They aren't dangerous, unless they grow too fast or interfere with another bodily system. And since there are so many, as you can see, it would be impossible to remove them all."

Suddenly, I have so many questions—treatments, options, probability, the normalcy of my little girl's future life. He patiently answers every one of them. "We just have to keep an eye on these tumors," he concludes, "and see what they do. Some vascular anomalies grow, some shrink, and some just stay the same. Every single case is different." An extended waiting game, I realize. I will be the watchman far, far longer than just today.

Sometimes I wonder about the things God allows us to endure. I no longer question His goodness, and after all the personal interaction my own soul has experienced with Him, I could not find an honest way to question His existence. I've walked with Him all my life; I don't know how I'd undo that. What I do question, however, is His involvement. Why does He spare some—heal some and not others? Are there real reasons? Or does He simply have to allow biology to run its course? I know He doesn't have to, because sometimes, every now and then, He does intervene. Otherwise, though, it seems He mostly sits back and allows it. Why is this? Is it fair? Did He ever say it would be fair?

We are waiting in post-op now, and I see a miniature stretcher being wheeled our way with my sweet Brooke on top of it, clutching her favorite dolly that they allowed her to bring into surgery with her. "Delivery!" the nurse announces cheerfully, and Brooke is in my arms before the stretcher has even come to a halt. She's awake, but still very groggy. "Mommy," she says softly, and I can't help it—I come apart, I come undone. "Hi, sweetie," I whisper into her sweaty hair, "Mommy loves you so much. So much," I repeat through my tears. I pat-pat-pat my hand on her little round tummy, imagining all the tumors, invisible to my eye, that I've just learned reside right underneath her skin. How could someone so perfect be full of so many problems? It's a hard idea to adjust to. I wish the blue tang were here to soothe me now with his rhythmic swimming, but he isn't.

In the days and weeks that follow, we break the news of Brooke's lymphatic tumors over and over, to our friends, family, acquaintances, church members, and Facebook community. I lose count of how many times I explain the tumor system that I barely understand myself. People are not satisfied when I admit, "I don't know what they're going to do yet," and neither am I; but that's the right answer for now.

"How are you guys doing?" they all ask me. "How do you feel?" And I know it's strange, but I can't help it—every time, I say, "Thankful. We are so thankful." I've talked to other parents who've spent time in those children's hospital hallways, some of them a lot of time, months and months, and they all say the same thing: "When we look around and see all the other kids here, when we consider how much worse it *could* be, we just feel thankful for our smaller problems." Friends tell me I'm brave, strong, faithful, heroic even, for feeling thankful. But they don't understand. They haven't been there and seen the bald heads and waited for the morning on the city walls. They don't know that "thankful" is the natural response, that "thankful" is the only way a mommy *could* feel when she gets to bring her baby girl home with her.

"Even if He doesn't," Lord, *"even if He doesn't." We are not as strong as they think we are, but we will take the good from You,* and *the bad, and we will trust You to somehow carry us through.*

IN CASE YOU GET SIX MINUTES TO YOURSELF: STUDY GUIDE

1. Have you ever sent a child or a loved one into a surgical procedure? How did you feel? What were your thoughts while you waited? How strong was your courage? Did your loved one get to come home with you, or not? How did that change things?
2. Was the friend's advice to the author on the phone all wrong? Are there Bible verses to support the practice of expecting God to answer us? How do we balance this with stories that show us He doesn't have to?
3. Read the story of the fiery furnace in Daniel chapter 3. Why were these men willing to serve God even if He didn't save them?
4. Have you wrestled with a "No" from God or a hard hand of fate dealt to you lately? Have you felt like God doesn't love you when He allows bad things to happen to you?
5. What is the secret to having faith through life's deepest tragedies?
6. If a tragedy came to you today, how would your own faith stand up to it?

Face to the Sun

M ommy! Why are you just standing there like a statue with your eyes closed?" my six-year-old exclaims from behind me. "Are you OK?"

It is late January, and we are walking around Lake Padden because the sun actually appeared. That's what Seattleites do: no matter how frigid the weather is, when the sun debuts in winter, you *go outside*—just go—take your whole family and rush outdoors for frantic vitamin D consumption.

On this particular day, my boy caught me standing at the end of a small pier, head thrown back, eyes shut, face tilted up to the sun in gratitude. Just. Can't. Move.

"Are you gonna keep walking down the trail with us, Mommy?" he suggests while riding his bike around in circles at the end of the pier.

Yes—I want to—I intend to—keep walking, but for the moment I am stuck here, riveted. I just can't get enough of this warmth on my skin. I'm bingeing on the sun's rare visit, decompressing my soul from the block of gray days we've already endured, and stocking up for the many long months of rain that I know are still ahead.

Sensing my need to stay in this moment of sun worship, my husband calls, "Come on, kiddos! Let's let Mommy have a quiet moment with her good friend the sun! She can catch up to us in a bit."

The crunch of bike wheels on the gravel and baby-booted feet against stroller sides picks up and then fades away behind me. I am alone at the water's edge. Sighs of deep contentment escape me. My head is still thrown back, eyes closed in delight, face lifted toward the afternoon sun.

I want to orient myself toward You in this same way, Jesus—eyes upwards, facing full into Your light whenever and however You appear. I want to position myself to soak up Your illumination the very second it's available. Let me be undivided, my Father. Help me to always be aware of Your Presence, and when I sense it moving among us, let me leave all with reckless abandon and find solace in the warmth of Your love. Don't let me miss those moments when You shine forth. Don't let any parade of dark days hide Your hope from me. And once You have set me ablaze in Your fire, make me a conduit to pass that flame on to others. Help me to be wholly drawn to You, heart and soul—always searching, ever seeking, face to the Son.

"The light shines in the darkness, and the darkness has not overcome it" (John 1:5, RSV).

IN CASE YOU GET SIX MINUTES TO YOURSELF: STUDY GUIDE

1. What has the weather of your life been like lately—sunny skies, dark days, chilly winds of change?
2. What does it mean to orient ourselves to seek Jesus, or to have our face to the Son? How can you do this?
3. Read John 1:1–5. What is the meaning of verse 5: "The light shines in the darkness, and the darkness has not overcome it" (RSV)?
4. Which areas of your life need God's light to shine through the darkness today?

Mom Texts

Sunday, 10:28 P.M.

Angela: Make it home OK?

> **Melissa:** We made it home from the beach right at sunset. It felt all emotional and significant—the sun setting on our summer and all. I'm really sad tonight. I don't want to send him off to school, I want to keep him :(

Angela: Summer is too short.

> **Melissa:** Look at me ironing uniforms at 10:30 P.M. for school tomorrow. Shame. But the best thing I have EVER done for myself? I went a little psycho before we left for the beach Friday and I cleaned the house spotless from top to bottom. So when we dragged in tonight exhausted and sand-covered and filth-crusted, we came home to a fresh clean house. It was A-Mazing. Love it. Never mind that we don't have any toilet paper, OR anything to pack in a lunch box . . . sigh. Win some, lose some.

Angela: Who needs toilet paper when you have $67 uniforms? Haha!

Melissa: Shut-UP! I'll call you tomorrow, OK?

Angela: OK

Monday, 9:06 A.M.

Melissa: Oh man I am fallin' apart! We dropped Caleb off for his 1st day of second grade. It doesn't seem to matter that I've done this already three times now—I still feel so sad to drive away and leave him there. He belongs with us! We went out to breakfast at a place that said "Family Café" and I just teared up because he's not here and our family isn't complete without him! I'm a mess. It's too stinkin' early for this kind of drama!

Angela: This is one of those sad rainy days you need to come over and visit while the rest of our kids play and we drink tea and eat chocolate to soothe our sad souls!

Melissa: Oh YES. But every day is one of those days.

Monday, 10:42 A.M.

Angela: Look at this pic I'm sending you—Seth bought me a mug from SB. I love it so much I didn't even get mad at him for spending money that we don't have on something that we don't need! Haha!

Melissa: Oooh! Love it!

Angela: It's such a nice day to be out
on the patio in the sun
drinking my tea while my girls
make bird nests out of grass
and eat graham crackers for
breakfast. I really need to go
grocery shopping . . .

Melissa: What?! It's sunny there? I thought you
said rainy? Oh you were talking about
me. So unfair. Gotta go—gonna call
you after lunch, OK?

Angela: Yep, OK.

Monday, 12:14 P.M.

Melissa: Sometimes the sound of silence in the
house is literally so beautiful it makes
me want to cry.

Angela: Well I fell asleep on the couch
and I just found the girls in
the coat closet spreading Vicks
vapor rub in their hair.
Perfect. They are so greasy,
I'm never gonna get it all out!

Melissa: Are you kidding me? WHERE do they
get these ideas?!

Angela: IDK!!!! But don't call me now!

Melissa: Silent house—always worrisome—
found the twins had pushed 2 chairs up
against the back kitchen counter and
were frantically shoveling handfuls of
cat food into their little mouths. SO.
DISGUSTING. They just sobbed and
sobbed when I pulled them away.
Really? It can't be THAT good!

Angela: HAHAHA!

Monday, 12:56 P.M.

Melissa: Well I am trying to play with Toby since Caleb's gone at school, and I'm learning all about their games: some superheroes have farting powers. Some turn people into stone (Narnia) or use the force (Star Wars) or there are 7 children who need a governess (Sound of Music). And of course Anna and Elsa (played by stuffed cats) turn everything to ice (Frozen). And there are water slides where mountain goats sniff your bottom....????? (No idea whatsoever!) Yeah. I don't think I am cut out to be a little boy.

Angela: Me neither apparently!

Monday, 1:30 P.M.

Angela: Here's my afternoon: Everyone and the dog greet you while you are on the pot. The burner decides not to turn off so I have to turn the whole breaker off and put lunch on hold until it decides to work again when I turn the breaker back on. And of course everyone is crabby and starving. Plus I tried forever to send one email for work since someone still hasn't got their tickets and outlook mail won't let me send email from home! And everyone wants to be cuddled, or in my space to see what I'm doing, and I'm nursing until

the baby throws up over me
and a bunch of work papers!

Melissa: Typical Day! I am mopping the floor:
such a pointless use of energy. It will be
covered in food and mud again in ten
minutes flat.

Angela: Mopping? Huh. Never heard
of it ;)

Melissa: I just found a Christmas ornament hook
in the middle of the floor. Seriously? It's
September! I have swept and vacuumed
dozens of times since Christmas! And
yet, here it is, little devil.

Angela: They multiply!

Angela: I keep thinking I'll get things
done and then I don't. I hate
incompetence and I'm like
queen of it today. I'm just
sitting here holding this
stinkin' cute baby and she's so
cuddly and sweet—I want to
hold her for hours!

Melissa: DO IT lady! They are only little for
awhile. Enjoy her ☺

Angela: What was that poem from
your mom that you pasted
onto my fridge when Made-
line was first born?

Melissa: "Cleaning and scrubbing can wait till
tomorrow, for babies grow up we've
learned—to our sorrow. So quiet down
cobwebs, dust go to sleep, I'm rocking
my baby and babies don't keep."

Angela: Ahhhh! Now I'm crying!
Thanks a lot!!!

Melissa: You asked, woman!

Monday, 2:03 P.M.

Melissa: Taking a break from cleaning—what in the world are homemade hand dipped wax candles doing on your Pinterest account, woman?! Are you going greenie-homestead mama on me?

Angela: No no no . . . it's for work haha. I used to think it was cool to make shampoo and detergent and all but really, who has time for that?! What women are these?? I'm just happy if I can whip up a box of Mac n cheese!

Melissa: K. Let me finish dipping my candles and knitting this blanket before I split some wood, and then I'll call you about the weekend plans ;)

Angela: I see you are jealous ;)

Melissa: Nope. I'm holding my sweet son on my lap and we are getting ready to read some stories. Life is good here on this homestead.

Angela: ☺

Monday, 2:45 P.M.

Melissa: Time to go pick up my boy from school!

Angela: Yaaaayyyy!

Monday, 4:17 P.M.

Melissa: So there's this ice cream stand out in the country by the tulip fields that sells scoops as big as a softball—amazing ice cream too. So we decide, hey, it's the first day of school, let's celebrate, that will be a fun family thing to do. Except it was nap time. And apparently very hot, even in spite of the rain. And the ice cream melted all over every inch of the twins' bodies until they were sticky little screaming whining monsters. And then Toby and Caleb started whining about how cold they were, and did they HAVE to finish all this ice cream? And so they went to jump around in the parking lot, by the road. This lady next to us—who shamelessly, literally had been pointing and laughing at us the entire time, pipes up and says, "There are a lot of drunk drivers on this road, you know. Look at where your boys are standing." Oh I wanted to punch someone in the face. But we had also bought peaches and fresh raspberries and I didn't even have any hands for punching and my own ice cream was dripping all over ME. Total, epic, fail. For a total of—wait for it—$36. And then Wyatt pees himself. Soaked through the shorts, dripping down his legs into his shoes, mixing with the ice cream streaks on his knees, ankles and feet. What a joyful time.

Angela: Yessssss! Howell luck!!! Hahahahaha!!!!

Melissa: It was a Howell moment to remember!

Angela: K I'm sending you this.

video—Chloe absolutely refused to pick up her toys at bath time, and she ran out of the bathroom naked and screaming. This is the footage of the grand-scale tantrum—it was so epic I just had to share. Note that I was also hit several times, and called "stupid." What a sweet little darling she is!

Melissa: LAUGHING! OUT! LOUD!!! My boys keep begging to see it over and over!

Melissa: Sooooo—have fun with that, I'll call ya later. Really. I really AM going to call you today, believe it or not.

Monday, 5:00 P.M.

Angela: Seth just invited company over for dinner in an hour. There is not a single free space on any of my counters. My sink is overflowing with dishes. There's Vicks Vapor Rub handprints and smears on all the walls. Dog hair blanketing the couch. And toys cover every single inch of my floor. Think they'll notice?

Melissa: Naaah, that stuff will TOTALLY blend in. Call me when they leave, dishes queen!

Monday, 7:09 P.M.

Melissa: Mothering boys rant: I walk into MY bathroom and there's literally pee everywhere—all over the toilet seat, all over the floor, dripping down both walls, splattered across the back of the toilet, and pooling in the trash can beside the toilet. Dear Son is walking away innocently. "WHAT HAPPENED HERE?!!" I questioned. His innocent response: "I just turned my head, what?" NO. You do not turn your head. You do not EVER turn your head—you are holding a loaded weapon there and you watch that thing every single second it is firing!!! Every. Single. Second!

End rant. But still shaking my head. And cleaning like a total germophobe.

Angela: A loaded weapon?! Hahahaha!!! Sick!

Melissa: How was dinner?

Angela: Still here!

Monday, 8:17 P.M.

Melissa: 4 kids in the bath together and all of a sudden Wyatt gets very serious, reaches down into the water, and hands me something—a great big lump of soggy poop. "Poop in the bath!" I yell, and everybody jumps up screaming, flinging poop and poop water on sides and edges and carpet. What a disaster!

Angela: Oh my lands!

Melissa: I don't know who is more soaked after a bath—my kids, or me.

Melissa: Now stinky soaking wet Wyatt just escaped from the bathroom and so Caleb to be *helpful* DRUG HIM all the way back down the hallway into the bathroom. There is a full-body wet water and poop smear from my kitchen all the way to my bedroom. Yep. On my freshly mopped floors.

Angela: I was seriously just getting ready to call you! This day! LOL

Melissa: Classic first day of school. Just classic. One for the scrapbooks for sure. Oh we are WINNERS! I'll call you when everyone's in bed.

Angela: I'm holding my breath . . .

Monday, 9:23 P.M.

Melissa: OK. Nope. I have no personality left whatsoever—totally beat. If you try to talk to me now there's just gonna be this buzzing dead space on the phone, I cannot even string words together at this moment, I'm so serious.…

Angela: It's OK. I was just thinking the same thing.

Melissa: No but I feel bad. I honestly planned to call you all day to figure this weekend out. Why is life so insane?! I just feel bad that we didn't get to talk ☹

Angela: Melissa—we actually talked all day. Like, the whole day. It was way better than any 15 minute phone call. Have a good night, my friend.

Trying to have a devotional life during these crazy motherhood years feels a whole lot like trying to make time in the day to call my friend Angela. I have the best of intentions. I plan to spend a nice big chunk of time with God. I keep meaning to get to it. But life happens. So often—far too often—I don't get that time block. I end up feeling guilty about not "having a devotional life," forgetting that it is possible and just as valid to connect with Him on a moment-by-moment basis. It may not be exactly comparable to spending an hour in deep Bible study, or to seeking God's will in fervent prayer. Those things are still needed, and they will always have their place. But when that intensity of time and focus cannot be attained (which is more often than I care to admit), a simple, ongoing conversation with God throughout the day can feed the soul too.

This sporadic yet steady text-type contact with the Lord is similar to what the Bible refers to as praying without ceasing in 1 Thessalonians 5:17. The concept has always been a bit fuzzy to me. Even before I had four kids, a husband, and a house, a cat and a dog, a school and two churches, and a partridge in a pear tree—I still couldn't have fathomed praying every moment of the day. Now, that idea is almost laughable. It seems to be solely for monks and lonely grandparents, not busy women in the real world.

But the true invitation behind the verse is to recognize the nearness of God's presence in every moment.* It's not only an awareness of His company, but also a habitual turning of the soul towards His friendship. Just as I think of texting Angela whenever something funny, sad, meaningful, or mundane happens, I can train my heart to seek God in key moments as well.

An author once wrote a letter to Christian mothers that said, "Your compassionate Redeemer is watching you with love and sympathy, ready to hear your prayers and to render you the assistance which you need. He knows the burdens of every mother's heart and is her best friend in every emergency."† The first time I read these words, I was shocked at how seldom I turn to this waiting, watching God in my daily "emergencies," when all along He is standing by ready to help me. How many moments could I have called upon Him, and didn't? Why do I forget that He is available?

After that, when I could feel my anger rising, my temper flaring, or my courage waning, I tried to remember to simply plead, "Help me, Jesus! I need Your help." But I also endeavored to share the boring, simple happenings with Him too. I started to meet Him at the changing table. I talked about my small grocery budget and how disappointing it is when my clothes still don't fit. I regularly called on Him while loading the dishwasher as my twins simultaneously unloaded it just as fast. I felt more inclined to reach out to the Lord in the school pickup line or at the routine vet appointment. And even though these dozens of small, silent prayers did not feel like much of a devotional life, they kept me talking to my Savior all day long.

I'm trying to guide my children into this practice too (sometimes teaching them

---

* *Andrews University Study Bible*, 1 Thessalonians 5:17.
† Ellen G. White, *The Adventist Home* (Nashville, TN: Southern, 1952), 204.

is much easier than teaching myself). My husband and I pray for windows of opportunity in which we can train their hearts heavenwards. Last night when the descending garage door caught the edge of the wood project that my husband has been working on for four months and knocked his masterpiece to the ground in pieces, my boys felt crushed to see their daddy so devastated. "Let's pray for him," I suggested. "Let's talk to Jesus about this." Two weeks ago when my son came home from school spitting mad at a boy who destroyed his sand castle on the playground, I suggested, "Let's talk to Jesus about this boy." For two weeks we prayed for him, and today my son excitedly shared that out of the blue, the boy began protectively guarding their sandbox work instead of wrecking it. "Jesus changed his heart, Mommy!" Caleb exclaimed. "It's like he's a new boy!" I look for these moments. I pray for eyes to see them when they come, so that I can instill in my kids what I'm trying to instill in myself: the constant exercise of turning, turning, turning to Jesus.

I don't always remember this discipline—it's something I'm still learning, something I have to intentionally practice—and I fail often. But yet, at the end of many days of this chitchat with the Divine, I'm surprised to realize that God has been a part of the whole day. Together, these small snippets of silent prayers began constructing a conversation thread that never really needs to end. And that just so happens to really be—believe it or not—praying, without ceasing.

Be encouraged, busy momma: God is available anytime, anywhere. Yes—even in *your* schedule. Don't wait for that fairy-tale block of uninterrupted time. Just seek Him in any old ordinary moment you can.

IN CASE YOU GET SIX MINUTES TO YOURSELF: STUDY GUIDE

1. Who is the friend or relative that you most regularly share your life's details with? What types of things do you like to share?
2. What is your prayer life like at this point in your life? When and how do you pray?
3. What are the things in your life that make it difficult for you to pray?
4. How do you understand the idea of praying without ceasing?
5. Read 1 Thessalonians 5:12–24, where the context of the "pray without ceasing" verse is found. What other spiritual disciplines does the apostle recommend, and which of these do you most need to cultivate?
6. If you miraculously received a silent hour today just for prayer, what things would you want to talk to God about the most? Could you begin talking about those now?

Blurry

The outfits had been picked and purchased for this purpose alone. Four pairs of matching shoes were chosen with care (and much searching). Hair had been washed, combed, tamed, and twisted into tiny pigtails with ribbons. My own outfit had undergone a runway model-type decision process among my closest friends: "Does this scarf match better, or that one? OK, which sweater makes me look the thinnest? Boots or heels, hair up or down?" Even my husband prepared with a fresh haircut for this once a year family event, and I do mean event: the annual Christmas card photo.

When the day finally arrived, I arranged my polished little cherubs in a semicircle on the back deck overlooking the forest—the year's location of choice. The semicircle looked too contrived, so next we tried a line, and then a cluster, until finally the pose appeared just right. Greg set up the tripod with a remote, adjusted the lighting, and framed the scene. I took my place behind my children, the ten-second timer began flashing, Greg jumped into the shot beside me, and we both yelled in earnest, "Smile kids! Smile big for Daddy's camera!" *Flash. Flash. Flash.* A burst mode of twelve shots, and the moment was captured at last! Greg dashed behind the tripod to look at the picture, and sure enough, in spite of all my perfect planning there it was—the one consistent factor in every single family photo we have ever taken of the six of us: Wyatt was blurry.

I can't get an in-focus shot of Wyatt to save my life. At eighteen months old, he is one constant whirlwind of motion and energy and noise. Just tonight I tried snapping a picture of him pushing his tank across the floor, but it looks more like a painting that someone smeared their fingers through. Earlier this afternoon, I placed a cowboy hat on his head and thought for sure it would buy me at least four seconds of puzzlement, but no. He was tearing that hat off with gusto even before my camera captured the first photo. In sibling pictures, he's the fuzzy one—turning to giggle at his brothers or attempting to run off-camera. And he has ruined more darling twin shots with his sister, Brooke, by flailing his arms in front of her face than I could ever count. The boy simply cannot be still.

Neither, it seems, can I.

Sometimes my own life feels like one big blur of survival from holiday to birthday to school to doctor's office to mealtime to bedtime and back again. I am always running, and running late. There is constantly an urgent matter pressing, whether it be the next meal everyone is "starving!" for, the next appointment, the school pickup, or someone having a mini crisis. It is hard to split my attention between four kids, a husband, and a house. It is hard sometimes to just explain what I've done all day, or even all month, except to say that it's been a blur.

And yet, opposed to this mess of madness and mayhem that is life with littles, God calls me into His presence to be *still*. "Be still, and know that I am God," He invites (Psalm 46:10). As if I should know how to do that. Oh, I can be still—out cold on the couch during an accidental afternoon nap. But if I'm awake? My mind, and usually my body, are anything but still. I can be still when I'm hidden in my closet, eating the very last piece of chocolate in the house, while a little voice inquires from the bedroom doorway, "Mommy? Are you in here?" I can be still when the kids peek in to see whether I'm awake for the morning. But that's about all I know of being still. Am I supposed to find time alone (hahaha) to sit somewhere in solitude and silence (HAHAHAHA) for a spell? Well that's unlikely, except in the bathroom—no, wait, never mind, not even there. So what could a verse like that possibly mean for a mother with a life like mine?

The first thing I notice about this welcome to "be still" is that it was spoken by Someone who must know me well. Someone who knows that my frantic mind doesn't experience "still" very often. But Someone who knows that I need "still," and need it desperately, therefore calling me to it. The second observation implied in being still and knowing that He is God is that I am not. God, that is. I am not God. And while that may seem obvious to everyone else, I sometimes run around acting like I am God—trying to fix everything and save everyone and control whatever I can. Insisting on getting my way at all costs and being righteously offended when I don't. So I need to remember that there is a God in the universe, and I am *not* Him. This is particularly encouraging during the times I feel helpless, because when I come to the edge of all that I know, it's good to have the assurance that God's knowledge knows no bounds. But is there more to this elusive stillness God calls us to encounter?

Many scholars have linked this little verse back to a much older text, one that it may have even been quoting, in fact. You might find that in your Bible, Psalm 46:10 is chain referenced to Exodus 14:14, which reads, "The Lord will fight for you; you need only to be still." These words are spoken as the Israelites are smack up against the Red Sea's breaking waves, high cliff walls on both sides, Egyptian army advancing in hot pursuit behind them. They are trapped in sheer and utter terror, facing certain death.

But into this place of panic, when nobody can conceive of any way out whatsoever, Moses speaks calm over the crowd. "Do not be afraid. Stand firm and you will see the deliverance the LORD will bring you today. The Egyptians you see today you will never see again. The LORD will fight for you; you need only to be still" (Exodus 14:13, 14) And the story ends with God Himself parting the waters of the Red Sea, the Israelites walking right through to the other side, and God bringing the waters crashing down once more upon the Egyptian army who was, in fact, never seen again. The Lord absolutely did fight for them—He did everything, while they watched with jaws dropped.

People who know how to be still before the Lord possess the assurance that God can fight their battles for them. All the stress we wrestle with, all the fears that advance upon us, all the pressures that pursue us, are things that God is already prepared to fight. Nobody likes feeling trapped, but sometimes when we are completely out of options, we are exactly in a perfect position for God to step in and work wonders. It is interesting to note that the phrase "be still" is translated as "to cast down, to let fall, to relax your hands." Being still before the Lord sometimes means simply letting go.

This is good news for those of us in mommyland, who find stillness and quiet hard commodities to come by. Because it means that even if our surroundings are in chaos, our souls can be anchored deep in the stillness that comes from certainty in God's power. I like to imagine God opening up a brand-new way through my troubles that never existed before. It is fun to picture million-gallon waves of grace burying all the scars I'd like to leave behind. I can't "be still" while God mops my floors or changes the diapers or cooks dinner for me—I still have to do these things. But I can be still in the midst of them, because I know that God will see me through.

I continue to wish I could find more time to be still before the Lord. But I've come to realize that what I crave even more than a moment of soul-stilling quiet is to be free—free from all that burdens me. And that's exactly why God calls us into His presence: in the submission of stillness, when we finally allow Him to fight for us, we can go out with hearts full and free. God wants this for me, and He wants this for you.

Have things been blurry in your life? Are you carrying the world's woes upon your shoulders? Be still, sister; you don't have to be God—Somebody infinitely capable already has the job. Are you flanked by cliffs of impossibility, armies of cares closing in? Be still, friend; the Lord knows how to fight for you.

IN CASE YOU GET SIX MINUTES TO YOURSELF: STUDY GUIDE

1. Is there somebody in your family or circle of friends who always ruins a good picture? How do you feel about them when you look back over the photos?
2. Read Psalm 46 and Exodus 14:13, 14. Why is it so hard to be still before God?

3. Does God promise to fight every battle for us, or are there some we must face ourselves?

4. How is it possible for one's heart to be stilled in the midst of activity and busyness?

5. What armies are advancing against you right now? How would you want God to fight for you in your current situation?

6. What areas in your own heart need to be stilled by God today?

The Office

I t's the clean couch that truly soothes me. My husband insists on leaving a few lights on all night long in his office. So when I am awakened in the night by a baby's cry and I go stumbling down the hall toward the nursery, I pass by the dimly lit office. If the maroon blanket covering the futon is spread without wrinkles, and if the two green pillows are propped at equal angles in opposing corners (this moment brought to you by the letters *O, C,* and *D*), and if no other clutter can be seen on the floor or around the couch, my soul is strangely, deeply comforted by the clean and calm, empty room. Juxtaposed with the screams of a hungry infant, this quiet room of books and order speaks sweet peace to me.

But if my boys leave, say, roughly 563 Hot Wheels cars or a miscellaneous pile of random clothing lying on the floor, or if my husband finally gets the mail out of the mailbox that month (he has the only key—let's blame him) and has it stacked in piles all around—these things literally and physically stress me out. Even though it's well past midnight and I may not even remember my own name, somehow I am still acutely aware of how the clutter in the office affects me. I can feel the tension. My inner perfectionist voice begins whispering that I really need to pick up those 563 cars and organize the mail—no matter that it's nearing 3:00 A.M. Who can sleep with a mess like this? Surely this room represents not only the state of the whole house but probably the state of my life as well!

That's why it makes such a difference when the office is clean and tidy as I go by. It's a spot of calm in an otherwise stressful night. Though there are screams of panic very nearby, there's a haven of peace peeking at me through the door. Because of that one room, I don't feel like my entire house is falling into chaos. The only pressure I put on myself is to feed the wailing child, and my inner perfectionist can congratulate itself on a job well done.

Heaven, to me, is the light left on in the clean office. It's a promise of peace in an otherwise frantic world. It's the spot of calm when stress and chaos are the realities to be found all around. And it represents the one area of my life that I allow myself to believe is totally taken care of—I *can't* do this job well enough, I *can't* clean this mess, but Jesus has done it for me. I may have to face a lot of craziness down here. But one day soon, there will be nothing left to panic about. Someday we won't have to live with today's pain and suffering. Looking down the hallway of time through the crack into heaven's door, I spy what my soul truly screams for: a better reality.

IN CASE YOU GET SIX MINUTES TO YOURSELF: STUDY GUIDE

1. What things in your own household bring you peace?
2. What things steal peace from you?
3. What part of motherhood could you compare to heaven right now?
4. How can the certainty of a better place in the future help you with your particular struggles today?

Application

"Describe yourself using a few sentences to explain: Who are you?"

The application question stared back at me from the blank page, and I did not know how to answer. A few sentences? Who am I? On the one hand, a few short sentences seem impossibly short to capture all that I am. On the other hand, I'm still answering this question for myself—who am I? Every day, with every choice, I address this question, and I'm still discovering its answer, still crafting its outcome.

Who am I?

I am a mother of four kids, a mother of twins, the wife of a pastor, and a pastor myself. I am the daughter of two amazing parents, the sister to three siblings. I am an auntie and a grandma (just kidding—just making sure you're with me). I am a writer, a harpist, an animal lover, and an outdoor enthusiast. I'm funny and fun and adventurous, spontaneous and bubbly and often happy. I am a woman of faith. I am a girl in love with sunsets and oceans and the starry night sky. I am a traveler. I'm a swimmer and a cook. I'm also story-reader, diaper-changer, owie-kisser, toddler-dresser, pigtail-stylist, and family chauffeur. I am a dreamer but not a planner. I'm faithful but not constant. I am found but still searching. I am me.

Because it's so hard to sum up ourselves as mothers and women, I asked myself, How does God sum me up? What would He say about me in answer to the question above? The list I found in the Scriptures was *so* much better than the one I made on my own. There is a remarkable difference too. My list was largely based on what I contribute and produce. But God's list is about my worth to Him, completely independent of anything I do or say.

In case you've been asking the same question, or in case you need a reminder today, here is the list. Don't listen to what the world tells you that you are, or even to what your failures summarize you as. Fasten yourself, instead, to who God says you are.

I Am Who God Says I Am:

I am His own (Isaiah 43:1).

I am His joy (Hebrews 12:2).

I am His work of art—His poem (Ephesians 2:10).

I am lovable (Jeremiah 31:3; John 3:16).

I am beautiful because of my heart (1 Samuel 16:7).

I am precious (Isaiah 43:4).

I have infinite worth (Matthew 10:29–31).

I am worth chasing after (Luke 15).

I am worth saving just as I am (Romans 5:8).

I am someone He knows completely, and yet He still loves me (Psalm 139).

I am someone He celebrates (Zephaniah 3:17).

I am a life He began a good work in (Philippians 1:6).

I am important, useful, and needed (1 Timothy 4:12).

I am someone He has plans for (Jeremiah 29:11).

I am someone He's coming back for (John 14:1–3).

I am worth His life (John 3:16).

IN CASE YOU GET SIX MINUTES TO YOURSELF: STUDY GUIDE

1. How would you summarize yourself in answer to the question, "Who am I?"
2. What are your favorite traits? Your least favorite?
3. Is your worth based more on what other people think about you, how you think about yourself, or what God thinks about you?
4. Which items in the list above mean the most to you, and why?

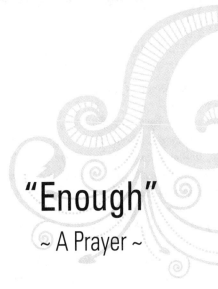

"Enough"

~ A Prayer ~

I *am not sure why I always come to the white pages of blank books to talk to You, Father, but here I am again, seeking You in these first soul-sighing quiet hours of Sabbath. There is so much vying for attention in me tonight: the holidays, church programs, parenting struggles, writing ideas, Christmas lists, cards, parties, menus, and more. I become consumed with all these crazy meaningless things, and I can't believe how often I totally forget You. How can I attempt these motherhood years without You? Why would I even dare? But I do. All the time.*

Always, Father, I keep coming back to that same solitary realization: I am not enough.

I am too small for this job. I had such a great mother, but somehow I don't think I've become one—I am selfish and distracted and sometimes so absent. Absent, ha—that's a funny word to choose because in reality I am never "absent." I am with my children almost every waking minute of every day. They are never absent from me, but I still feel absent so often. What I guess I mean is that I don't fully feel present. I get lost on Facebook, Pinterest; lost in texts, lost looking for something out there in the world to make me feel . . . significant. I guess those moments of checking out wouldn't bother me so much if I felt certain I was already doing enough. Oh that awful word! Enough.

What is enough, anyway? What does it even look like, and what does it mean, since I spend my life chasing after it? I don't care what it looks like to other people, Lord. I just want to know what it looks like to You. *What do You hold me accountable for? What do You expect? Because sometimes it feels like You expect a lot, Father—giant, heavy, enormous things like molding characters and shaping souls and training up a child ×4 in the way they should go. Are these real weights You've laid on me? I think they are. People say they are.*

I know that no one can save my kids but You, Jesus. But for some reason, I still feel so responsible to teach them all the right things, show them all the right ways, and love them completely at all the right times and moments . . . wow. How can I do that? I'm still working on loving myself!

How much do You really expect out of me, God? Which expectations come from You, which originate from the world, and which are just webs I've spun for myself? What is "enough" before You, in motherhood? And if I were doing "enough," how would I know? Because I want to know, I have to know; if I don't know, I'm afraid I will mess it all up. So many things that happen to me all day long are simply reminders that I am not doing "enough." Oh, God—what is enough?

You are Enough. I know that. I know Your strength is made perfect in my weakness—but wait—how does that work in motherhood? Don't my weaknesses negatively affect my children? How can invisible You step in and fill up all the gaps where I'm deficient? How is that even possible? You can't come and play with one boy when I've pushed him aside for other things all day. You can't comfort the crying baby when she's hungry. You can't ask the school son how his day went when I haven't spoken more than four sentences to him and they were all comprised of things like, "Put your socks on!" and "Sit down right now!" Who makes up for these things, God? You? How is Your power made perfect in these weaknesses? I just don't see it.

I don't know, Father. I know I start to feel endlessly unhappy in motherhood whenever I'm beating myself up for the things I'm not doing "enough" of. There are so many things I do right, though! People say all the time how sweet my kids are, how obedient, fun, kind, and happy. We have fun, we eat healthy, we spend time in nature, we learn about You. But my pile of shortcomings feels larger than the real-life laundry piles in this house—and that's pretty large. There's got to be a way to live in grace somewhere in the middle of all the expectations—real or imagined. Teach me that, Father, if it even exists. Maybe the day will never come when I feel like I'm complete. I'm always trying to do the right things, but I'm always going to fail. Guaranteed.

I will never be enough, will I?

It's a hard thought, but it's true. I don't even know what I need to ask for on this journey of motherhood, let alone what I'm supposed to do. But You know. Your Spirit interprets my cries and knows what I'm trying to ask for, even when I myself am not sure (Romans 8:26). Which means—You're partnering with me, God! You're walking me through this. Oh, how I need You. I'm terrified by the significance of this task. Help me, help me, help me, help me, help me—I could fill up a whole page of "help mes," and it wouldn't be enough. And, there's that word again.

Maybe I don't have to be enough?

What if all I really needed to do was just put myself into Your hands, every day, and go from there? Granted, it might not change much around the house. But maybe I'm actually supposed to know that I'm not "enough"; maybe none of us are enough, and that realization is there on purpose to propel us to seek You. Well then, here I am. Seeking You. Calling out to You, just like always. Laying the wreckage of myself before You: Here I am: forever not enough.

I'm the wayward son in rags, limping down the road home, penniless and starving and smelling like pigs. I've spent all You gave me. I've made fools of us both. I only intend to come begging for mercy. But I see You, Father—there in the distance, on the road up ahead. What? You've been waiting for me? Now I imagine—no—it can't be! You are running, faithful Father! Running to meet me, closing in the gap between us. You don't wait for me to make it all the way to You. You never expected me to cover the whole distance on my own. All along, You always intended that if ever I came heading Your way, You would close in the rest of the road with Your own divine speed. And it doesn't matter that I am not "enough," it's not important that I am filthy and frail, because You've put Your own robe over my rags, and we're walking home together.

So. This is how Your power meets our weakness, Father. Even when we are still "a long way off," when we are anything but enough, as long as we are coming toward You, You will run the rest of the way to meet us. In motherhood, in parenting, in every struggle—all we need to do is head Your way, start toward You. We may not get very far, and our best efforts may stink like swine, but that's OK. You'll see us coming, and You'll escort us home; that's Your promise and Your joy.

Oh. I see! The shaping of their hearts is actually Your business. My God—help me to learn to see it that way. Show me how to teach them and love them as best I can, but help me remember that You do the most important work. You're not partnering with me—I am partnering with You!

I've been chasing the wrong thing. No more muscling to make myself better. Let me use all that energy instead to just seek You. I don't know how You're going to use my weakness, and I don't know how You're going to help my kids exactly, but what if I could just trust You to find them where they are? Because even if I mess everything up, You will still seek my children. You know the roads they are on, You've been waiting for them. You will do all the work that I never could have done anyway, God. Reach their little hearts, Lord. Teach them who Jesus is, if I fail to do so well. Teach them to love You if I can't. Create a desire in their hearts to serve You, because I know I can't do that. Save them, my God. Save my children, because I cannot. But You can—it's Your specialty, I know. You close in the gap, even when we are still a long way off.

Thank You for the freedom of not trying to do Your job anymore. I know You are already at work in their precious lives. Claim them as Yours, Jesus. And claim me too. After all these years, I still want to be Yours, Father. I'm still on the road home. Help me to throw myself into just being Yours and loving You—maybe that's the full sum of my work—because if I love You desperately, how could my kids ever miss it?

Ah, there is never enough time with You. But in that sentence, enough is finally a good word, because it keeps me coming back, ever returning for more of Your presence.

IN CASE YOU GET SIX MINUTES TO YOURSELF: STUDY GUIDE

1. Which areas of motherhood/marriage/Christianity/life make you feel like you are not "enough"?

2. Do you think the author of this prayer was too hard on herself, or are the feelings accurate—that nobody is ever enough?

3. In your opinion, what are the few most important jobs in motherhood?

4. Read the story of the prodigal son in Luke 15. Why was the image of the father running to meet the son so significant to the author? What does it tell you about how God treats sinners and people who are not "enough"?

5. In what ways do you need Jesus to make up the difference for you today? Which gaps in your family do you need Him to fill?

Wool Sweater

We spent the entire day under the desert sun—hunting for anthills with the kids, picnicking on blankets in patches of shade. My skin is rosy, my hair tangled from the incessant desert wind. I remember the quail walking along the walls, the cactus at my feet, the way my little boy's cheeks glowed red and damp. I lost track of how many times I needed to put on lip balm, apply sunscreen to tiny shoulders, or reach for another bottle of water. But there were some things we never needed even once . . .

Tonight at bedtime, rummaging through my suitcase in the dark room where my babies slept, my hand ran across a heavy wool sweater folded on the bottom. When I packed this sweater just a few days ago on a chilly gray Seattle afternoon, I first had the thought that I probably wouldn't need it here in the desert. But that immediately seemed crazy—I wear my gray wool sweater every single day. I take it and my kids' coats everywhere. I even have an extra sweater for each of them in the car, just in case one gets soaked, soiled, or lost—we need them that bad. We would freeze without them, I knew. So I packed them. My children's sweaters were all folded beside my wool sweater—four in a row, completely untouched and seeming utterly ridiculous now in the balmy dark room.

But I had forgotten what it was like to live in the sunshine.

I didn't recall what life is like in warm places, didn't remember that hot desert winds blow even at night. The still-toasty pavement makes even socks unnecessary, and a wool sweater is good only to be rolled up under one's head for star gazing. It's funny now to think that—from my Seattle standpoint—I couldn't imagine being warm enough to not need it.

I pack my pain around like this too. In a way, don't we all? We lug these heavy burdens to and fro every day—scars thick as wool—yet we are unable to imagine setting them down, leaving them behind. Won't we be naked if anger and resentment aren't here to protect us from more heartbreak? If we don't cloak ourselves in the failures and faults of the past, won't we soon find ourselves subject to them again? I think we all long for lighter loads and freer hearts, the same way a traveler likes to be free from extra unnecessary baggage. But we are scared—too scared—to leave it behind. We have forgotten what it was like to live in a place where armor is not needed.

What I want to remind myself tonight is that, although it's sometimes scary and difficult to forgive, to lay down, and to let go—it can also be just the thing that frees me enough to feel the sun on my skin again. To feel love and joy again, in the places of my heart that I've been barring and protecting like a policeman. Next time I come to the desert in the early summertime, I don't want to drag my wool sweaters with me—no matter what temperature Seattle is when I leave. And next time my heart is wounded, damaged, or hardened, I don't want to wear that pain like a permanent overcoat into my future either. I deserve the sun. My children deserve the sun. They deserve to know a mommy who is free, so I can somehow teach them to live free as well.

For everything, there is a season. There really *is* a time to hurt and grieve and allow anger to run its course. There's a time to wrap up in protective wool. But there is also a time to cast it off and give our hearts the chance to love and live again. I think the key is knowing the location of where we are. When you're in the rain? I say cover up. Protect yourself for a time. But when that sun comes back, have the courage to leave those heavy covers behind.

IN CASE YOU GET SIX MINUTES TO YOURSELF: STUDY GUIDE

1. What are the classic items you tend to bring on trips that always end up being unnecessary?
2. Why do people often hold on to pain instead of moving past it?
3. What significant personal "wool sweater" wound or burden are you lugging around right now? Why are you still carrying it? How is this burden affecting your family?
4. What would "life in the sun"—a.k.a. life without the burden—look like?
5. Read John 8:31–36. What is the truth that could set you free today?
6. Are you ready to be free of that burden? What do you need to do?

Bailing Water

I see him there in the bottom of the boat, collapsed in exhaustion, because that's exactly where I'd be today, too. The waves crash over the little boat's edge, and I realize He must be soaking wet by now, but He's still asleep. That's what soul-tired looks like, and I know it well. Even as He's trying to escape to the uninhabited other side of the lake to get some peace, other boats follow Him, like children trailing me through the house when I just need a moment of quiet.

On these waters, the wind sweeps wildly down through the mountain gorges along the eastern shore, and just then a furious tempest bursts out upon the lake. The waves are lashed into a frenzy by the howling winds, and they swamp the boat with seawater over and over and over. The disciples spiral down into a panic—which reveals a lot, because these men have spent their lives on the sea. These hardy fishermen have guided their boats through many rough storms, no doubt. But here they are, afraid for their lives, and rightly so, it seems. Except that they forgot about Jesus—and I do this too. Inundated with waves of stress and storms of chaos, I forget that Jesus is on board. I, too, battle the storm alone.

In the illumination of the lightning's crack, they suddenly catch a glimpse of Jesus' face—it is peaceful. He sleeps soundly on a sopping cushion, completely undisturbed by the disaster. Even this seems familiar to me, because I've often resented my God seemingly asleep through my darkest nights.

We don't know which one of them shook His shoulders at last, accusing Him, "Teacher, don't You care if we drown? Save us Lord, for we perish." We are told that never has a soul uttered that cry unheeded,* that this is a cry Jesus always hears and responds to.

I don't know what the disciples imagined Jesus would do that night on the stormy sea. I know they were afraid for their lives, I know they woke Him up in desperation,

---

* Ellen G. White, *The Desire of Ages* (Mountain View, CA: Pacific Press®, 1898, 1940), 335.

but what did they hope He would do? Because when my God stood up, rebuked the winds, and said to the waves, "Quiet! Be still!" and they *obeyed*—clouds rolling away and stars shining through—when this happened, the Bible says that the disciples were shocked. They didn't expect this. I don't know what they expected, but it certainly wasn't this.

I think they wanted Jesus to help bail water. I think they hoped He would grab an oar and swiftly row them to shore. They wanted menial help, they expected only minimum participation from Jesus. "Just help us bail water, Jesus, just help us keep this boat afloat." But Jesus stood up and shut down the whole storm, and the disciples were terrified (*amazed* is a good translation).

How many times have I done this? I ask for God to simply bail some water in my life, when all along He has the power to actually stop the storm entirely. I forget this. I underestimate Him. I waste time heaving tiny buckets, when I serve a God who controls the sea. Oh, I've wasted *so* much time bailing water. Gone through so many angry days because God doesn't seem to be bailing water too. I pray stilted prayers, hoping He can just help me survive, just get me to shore. But I forget I am in life's boat with God who is able to rescue me from my situation entirely.

What storms are raging in your life today, tired Mommy? Does God seem asleep at the stern? What kind of miracle have you been asking for? Have you just begged Him to bail some water, or have you asked Him in the fullness of faith to calm the storm completely? He's still the same God. He can calm any storm you're facing. "Be still my soul: the waves and winds still know His voice who ruled them while He dwelt below."*

IN CASE YOU GET SIX MINUTES TO YOURSELF: STUDY GUIDE

1. If you imagine yourself in this story of Jesus and the storm, which of the characters would you be and what would your personality type be doing—huddling in fear, barking orders, rowing to shore, or something else?
2. When was the last time you wondered whether God is asleep in your life? Is He?
3. What do you think the disciples expected Jesus to do when they woke Him up?
4. Do you believe that God can calm your storm entirely? Have you been asking for this? Why or why not?
5. Which storms do you need to hear Jesus' voice ringing through today?

---

* Katharina von Schlegel, "Be Still My Soul," trans. Jane Borthwick, *The Seventh-day Adventist Hymnal* (Hagerstown, MD: Review and Herald®, 1985), no. 461.

Hiding

The first thing I noticed was the blood. Blood on the kitchen floor, blood drops peppering the carpet, wadded-up paper towels soaked in blood. I didn't know where he was yet, but I knew he was hurt.

We have rules in our house about not playing with knives. And we've had to add other rules, like not playing with razors. Or saws. Or axes, or drill blades, or anything else that a boy could possibly find in Daddy's garage that is sharp enough to cut him. These rules have been in place in our family for a long time—since the first boy was old enough to push a chair against the kitchen counter and pull a butcher knife out of the knife block. But just because we have these rules doesn't mean they are always followed.

I imagine that's why the bleeding boy hid from me—because he knew his spear-carving had broken the rules. I suspect he tried to patch up his own cuts so that he might avoid having to admit that he'd disobeyed.

But I wasn't thinking about his disobedience at all when I happened upon the bloody evidence. All I could think about was finding him and making sure that he was OK.

Finding him didn't turn out to be too terribly hard. After searching in his room, the basement, and the backyard, I eventually found him hiding at the edge of the woods near the blackberry bushes. I hurried over to his hunched little body and saw immediately that the wound was on his hand. He had tried to cover it up—a crisscross patchwork of about twelve Band-Aids spread over his sliced-up palm. But the blood was still soaking through. He was hurt badly.

"Sweetie!" I exclaimed as I led him into the house. "What are you doing out here? Why are you hiding from Mommy? Why didn't you tell me you were hurt?" I questioned him.

He hung his head in shame. "Because, Mommy," he sheepishly admitted, "I just knew you'd be mad that I used Daddy's big knife to make my spear."

"Listen to me," I ordered, bending down on one knee in the wet grass so I could look him straight in the eyes. "I don't care what you've done wrong—when you are hurt, you come to me. Mommy is a safe place, Mommy will always help you if you are hurt, honey. You don't run away from Mommy when you are in trouble, you run *to* me. OK?"

He nodded his head, the first signs of relief showing on his little face. "OK, Mommy," he agreed. "OK." I took him inside and began to peel off ill-placed Band-Aids.

Perhaps the most important choice I can make in my walk with God is whether I come *to* Him or run *from* Him when I'm in trouble. I don't sneak knives out of the garage to whittle spears with, but I am pretty proficient at cutting up my own heart. I've been known to run and hide when I'm angry at Him, doubting Him, or discouraged by Him. But when my soul is torn and bleeding, when all the bandages I paste on don't come anywhere near healing my wounds, at that time hiding is the worst choice I can make. When my life is falling apart, and especially when my relationship with God is threatened, it's then that I need to run to Him most. It's the times I'm in trouble that I need to turn to God the most.

I'd wager that the single best predictor of a faith that won't be shredded during trials is the determined resolve to come to God with everything, always, no matter what. When I reread through my old prayer journals and think back on the faith struggles I've fought through, it's amazing to realize that the hardest times in my walk with God took place when I was running from Him. Even when the battles were fierce, even when they concerned God Himself, if I was turning to Him, I was somehow OK.

If your heart is bandaged and bleeding today, if life's edges have been too sharp, don't stay away from God until you've got it all figured out. Seek Him, find Him, run to Him instead—He's waiting with the healing that only He can truly give.

IN CASE YOU GET SIX MINUTES TO YOURSELF: STUDY GUIDE

1. When was the last time you or one of your children hurt themselves significantly? Was the tendency to ask for help or to heal it on your own?
2. When you're angry or struggling with God, are you more likely to come to Him or run from Him? Why?
3. How does the simple act of telling the Lord about our problems start to heal us? Does it always work? Why, or why not?
4. Have you been hiding from God in any way?
5. Which struggles do you need to bring before God today?

New Friend

S o, where are you from?" the woman asked me as the mixer game bustled through the group around us.

Where am I from? That's a great question—I have lived all over: California, Arizona, Nebraska, Michigan, the Marshall Islands, and even Ohio for a summer . . . I don't even know where I'm from, or where I'm going to end up either. What would you think about me if I told you that?

"California," I respond. "I grew up in California, and then my family moved to Arizona during high school. Where are you from?"

It's awkward to make eye contact with her because she never looks away! Do I look away too much? Do I seem uncomfortable? Nervous? Insecure? Am I?

"I grew up around here."

Wow. To live in the same area you grew up in, what would that even be like? Oh no, it's silent. What should I ask her now? Wait, she is talking . . .

"So you mentioned the other week that you and your husband were both trained as pastors . . ."

Oh no, why did I disclose that? People always treat me weird when they find out I'm a pastor. I should have stayed anonymous. Is she going to treat me weird now? Is she afraid I'll be judgmental? Will she expect me to be holier, somehow pastorlike? I just want to be treated like a normal mom.

"Where did you guys meet?"

The nerdy guy in the back row, plaid shirt, glasses, wavy swooping hair bangs, who shared his cappuccino with me.

"Oh, we met in college—in Greek class actually!"

(Nervous laughter.) Do I seem like a nerd now? Because I took Greek? It's not like I remember much of it . . .

"What about you, where did you meet your husband?"

She's still staring at me—is there something in my teeth? Do I look fat standing like this? I bet my baby pooch is showing. Maybe I should stand up straighter? Why do I have such terrible posture?

"We met at church," she begins, "but we've had to leave that church recently because of some personal drama. Actually, I really appreciated your testimony last month because I'm going through a *lot* right now myself."

Oh! She liked my testimony! That was such a vulnerable experience; I've been wondering what people think of me now. How wonderful to know she was blessed! I feel useful, I did a good job, I said something helpful that mattered to someone . . . I'm significant . . .

"I'm sorry to hear that," I say.

Does she want me to ask about it? I should ask about it. Or is it personal? Am I supposed to read her cues? Is she giving any cues? I really like her, so I want to say the right thing. Wait. Look at that woman standing behind her, she is so-o-o-o-o skinny and put together, wow, and that thick, long, wavy hair! I want to look like her. I need to go to the gym more. Why aren't I disciplined like other women? Oh—I am talking to someone!

"So much has happened all at once here, I just don't know what God's trying to teach me."

The open-ended statement. She is waiting for my answer. I don't know what God's trying to teach her! I hardly even know what God's trying to teach me. I know I'm a pastor so I'm supposed to know. But I don't. There is so much I still don't know. Am I good at this job? Maybe I'm all wrong for this job. What can I say that will help her?

"It sounds like you are still in the middle of the story," I suggest. "We often don't understand the lesson until the end."

I suddenly feel for her. I'm starting to care about her. She is a really genuine person, and I think I could like her a lot. But mostly I want her to like me. Am I likeable? Do I seem too confident? Conceited? Too eager? Do people want to be friends with me? Why have I had a hard time making friends in this new town?

Later in the morning, as I'm driving home from the Mothers of Preschoolers (MOPS) meeting, I'm thinking about this conversation with my new friend. I'm struck by how quickly we hit it off and began sharing our hearts and our struggles. But I'm also impressed by how difficult it can be to open up to a stranger, to risk rejection by putting myself out there when I have no guarantee that they even like me in the first place. What if they see my obvious flaws and annoying traits (which definitely exist)? I'm always wondering whether enough of my good qualities will surface in time for me to still come across as a desirable friend.

Wait—am I still in ninth grade? Actually, it seems like I had way more confidence in high school than I do now! What is it about motherhood that threatens to destroy our confidence?

Several months earlier, on a trip back to Arizona, I met my high school friends Penny and April for lunch at Macayo's (which is, by far, the best Mexican restaurant on the earth), and we talked about this very thing. Crunching chips and salsa and savoring unrivaled Baja sauce over green corn tamales, we commiserated on how motherhood has turned out to be harder than we expected.

"What makes it so hard?" someone asked.

"I think it's that I feel so bad at it," I suggested, and then we all fell silent, because sometimes truth needs a moment to sink in.

"Why are we always second-guessing ourselves?" April asked. "We are all clearly amazing women!"

"We can see that about each other, but it's hard to see it in ourselves," Penny clarified.

Into this dizzying search for identity, self-worth, and confidence in ourselves, the apostle Paul speaks a statement like solid ground after a stormy sea: "Being confident of this, that he who began a good work in you will carry it on to completion until the day of Christ Jesus" (Philippians 1:6). I've got to remember that I'm still a work in progress. Just like the dozens of half-started projects scattered around my house—baby books, memory frames, decorations, costumes, and clothes to mend—I am unfinished. But unlike those projects, which may lie around in varying states of completion forever, God intends to complete me. The ultimate culmination of His work in me will take place when Jesus returns. But until that time, each and every encounter with Him is moving me more toward fullness of character.

Long ago, Paul says, God began a good work in me: this is a truth I need to tether myself to. Even when I don't feel like there's much of anything good in me, even when I'm insecure and questioning my own worth, God isn't. He started something, set His plans for me into motion, and He's going to finish it. If God can love us in this imperfect, unfinished state, maybe we can learn to love ourselves in it too. And if we learn to love ourselves, rough and lacking though we may be, perhaps it just might be possible to truly value others under construction as well.

IN CASE YOU GET SIX MINUTES TO YOURSELF: STUDY GUIDE

1. What are the things you usually think and feel when you meet a new person? Do you compare yourself? Try to listen? Size them up? Try to make them like you?
2. Were you more confident in high school, or are you more confident now? What is the reason for the change?
3. How do you still struggle with value, identity, and self-worth?
4. Read Philippians chapter 1. What is the work that God has begun in you, and where do you see signs of His shaping and sculpting in your life?
5. How does it change your self-perception to know that you are unfinished? To know that one day you will be complete?
6. In which areas do you need the most assurance today?

Pastor's Wife

Hi, my name is Melissa, and I am a pastor's wife. No, I don't play the piano or lead children's church. No, I don't bring the best or even the most casseroles to potluck each week (actually, sometimes I don't bring anything). I don't have my husband's schedule memorized, so I won't be able to tell you whether he can speak for your event next week or not. What I can tell you is that if he speaks for your event, that's one precious night of the week he might have actually been home with his family, which we would lose. No, I don't always wear the right clothes, and if my pants are too tight, I promise it's not because I'm trying to be rebellious—it's because I'm pregnant again, or just gaining weight, and I can't afford to replace them right now. No, my family doesn't have worship three times a day, but we do our best to squeeze it in when we can. I hope it's not a predictor of how crazy my "pastor's kids" are going to turn out, but thanks for making me paranoid about that. And no, I didn't make those excellent chocolate cookies on the foyer table at church after the evangelism series last night. No, I didn't make the peanut butter ones either. Or the sugar cookies. Actually, I didn't make any cookies for that meeting. Why not? Oh—because I preached the series.

I am also a pastor myself. Not at the moment—right now I'm a stay-at-home mommy. But I am seminary trained and theologically indoctrinated to the gills, I assure you. Not that I ever use much of that training here at home—it doesn't take any theology to make a sandwich (it might take some to break up the fight about who took the mystery bite out of the sandwich, however).

As I mentioned, my pastor-husband Greg and I met in Greek class. When we were both eighteen years old and very young and naïve, we thought that the life of a pastor would be glamorous and exciting and important. We would be reaching and saving lost people! Hallelujah! We would change the world! We sincerely believed that going into the ministry was the very best use of our lives and our talents. We still believe that, by the way. And there are so many things to love about this life—oh, so many things! The thrill of dipping someone under the waters of baptism, the privilege of offering the last prayers before life-threatening surgeries, the honors of conducting weddings and baby dedications, and the joy of seeing God alive and active and moving in so many different lives. It's an amazing job; we were right!

However, I never could have known back then in college, when we accepted God's call into ministry, how deeply this job goes *against* the grain of who I am at my very core and of all the things I truly want out of life. I used to want adventure and change all the time. I liked moving every few years, meeting new people, and seeing the world. But once I had kids, there were dreams revealed in my heart that I never even realized I had: to settle down in a town and to be "from" somewhere, for example. Or to have our kids grow up in the same house with the same friends, to belong in a circle of lifelong mother friends, all raising our kids together. I wanted to plant a garden and just watch it grow year after year. (Pastor's wife inside joke: Don't plant bulbs. You will be sure to get another call before they ever bloom.) I didn't realize we would have to give up those things all the time. I don't even know how many times we have moved or how many churches we have pastored—I guess I'd have to count. I also didn't realize that I would want the ability to choose my own church, one that really fits us and works for us, instead of being assigned to one.

After having a few kids and starting to feel significantly emptier than I did as a college student, I started to realize that I didn't want to always be the one spiritually feeding someone else. I wanted to be fed myself. I wanted to find friends who would be real and honest with me—nobody seems to want to be truly honest with a pastor's wife. Why not? I think they only want you to know the good things about them.

We were in a difficult church when I started having these thoughts, and as my discontentment grew deeper and deeper, a bitter root began to grow in me that I allowed and even cultivated. Right around this same time, a lot of drama broke out in one of our churches. There was fighting, there were threats, there were secret meetings to get us fired held in the homes of friends I cared about. Things got uglier and nastier as we tried to continue ministering to unhappy people. Finally, when we understood that a sense of peace would never be reached, we knew it was time for us to leave. Again.

When that realization hit us, something significant broke open inside of me. The bitter root blossomed into a fully poisonous flower, and I started to feel as though we had to give up too much for this life. The cost was too great. God asks us to give up too much, and He will continue to ask that. There's too much pain and loss, and we will never belong anywhere. I started asking dangerous questions: Is our sacrifice worth it? Does church ever really help anyone? What are we giving up our lives for?

Though the majority of mothers aren't pastor's wives, I think that every single mother in any profession can identify with the feeling of having given up so much. I mean, just think of what we have given up for motherhood—many of us gave up jobs and careers and the opportunity to really be "somebody" out there in the world, to stay home in sweatpants with tiny people. Or we gave up quiet afternoons in sweatpants with tiny people to slave away at jobs we hate, so that we can provide for them. We gave up our sleep. We gave up our bodies and our figures. We gave up a lot of our freedom—the ability to go where we want whenever we want. We gave up our sanity, our ability to go to the bathroom in peace, the chance to finish a sentence or think an uninterrupted thought. Some of us even gave up our dreams, and we lost ourselves and our identities altogether in motherhood. The cost is great. We have given up so much.

For some reason, at this difficult time in our lives, while I was angrily packing boxes and blaming vicious people, I was drawn to the story of Hannah in the Bible. Hannah was the mother of Samuel, one of the greatest prophets who ever lived, but her story begins before Samuel, with her unable to have children. She cannot get pregnant—how well some mommies remember that feeling. The Bible says she begged God, she cried out to God "in bitterness of soul." I identified with that feeling immediately, the feeling of crying out to God in bitterness of soul. (Maybe you can identify with that too?) That phrase, "bitterness of soul," is only used exactly like that in the Hebrew one other time, in the book of Job. When Job has lost everything and he's scraping the boils on his skin, he cries out to God in "bitterness of soul." I wasn't scraping boils, but my resentment boiled furiously.

One of the first things that struck me deeply about Hannah's story was that this "bitterness of soul"—this is an OK way to come before God. It doesn't seem like it. It actually seems disrespectful or wrong. But we know that it's permitted because not only does God accept it from Hannah, He actually honors it: He gives her a baby. Which means that even though she was full of bitterness, the bitterness wasn't the truest thing about her. Her coming to God was the truest thing—she was still God's girl. We can come to God in bitterness, and He is able to see through that. Hallelujah! That was good news for this disgruntled pastor's wife.

I was tracking with this story, and I was encouraged by Hannah's raw emotion, until I reached the part of the story where she takes little Samuel to the temple, and she gives him away. This was right—she promised God that if He gave her a son, she would dedicate the child to God's work. But it wasn't right. Here she finally got this baby that she had wanted so desperately, and then she had to give him up. She had to give him back to God.

I just wanted to scream, because it seemed way too close to my story (the Bible has a way of doing that—of finding our stories). It rang true all over again that the cost is too great, and we have to give up too much to serve God. He asks us to give up the very things that matter most to us. It isn't fair! Oh, I was angry.

For some reason, though, I pushed on to the end of Hannah's story.

Hannah's story ends with Samuel ruling as the greatest prophet that Israel had ever seen, we know that. But her story also ends with Hannah herself having five more children after Samuel. When I read that little detail of her five other kids, it hit me suddenly. I have heard this story my entire life, and I have read it more times than I could even count, but somehow I never saw it before.

All at once I was convicted with full force that God replaces everything that we give up for Him, above and beyond. He doesn't ask too much. He doesn't leave us wanting. Every single thing that we give up for the Lord will return to us as a blessing five-hundredfold or more. Is this story a promise? Oh, I wanted it to be a promise. It was a promise to me that day. God may ask us to give up a lot. But He will never fail to replace it with more blessings than we could ever imagine. Hannah's five children picked up shovels then and dug resentment's roots out of my heart, and I thanked them. Gladly, I watched it go.

Pastor Case, one of my theology professors at Union College, taught me many years ago to pray a prayer that asks, "God, give me what You know I would want if I could see the end from the beginning as You can." I've prayed that prayer all these years, and I'm learning to believe that's exactly what God does for me. When I can't see why He's asking me to be someone, to go somewhere, to give up something more, He is weaving the tapestry of good plans that He's fashioned for me.

I don't know what you have had to give up in life. But if you find yourself in that position today—in Christianity or in motherhood—of feeling like the cost is so great, of feeling like we have to give up so much, be encouraged. If you have been asking the question, "Is it worth it?" be comforted by the fact that whatever we give up for God or for our families in this life, God multiplies in blessings both here on earth and one day soon in heaven. So take heart. The cost is not too great, because the reward is far, far greater. Seeing my children and your children in heaven at the feet of Jesus one day? That will absolutely be worth every single last livin' thing that any of us have *ever* given up.

So press on, mothers. Step forward bravely, pastor's wives. It's worth it. What we are doing will be rewarded, more than our imaginations can even fathom.

(Now go make some casseroles for potluck—because I'm not bringing anything again this week.)

IN CASE YOU GET SIX MINUTES TO YOURSELF: STUDY GUIDE

1. Have you ever held a job or taken a position that turned out very differently than you had imagined it would? What happened?
2. Have you ever questioned whether or not it is worth it to serve God? What answer did you come to?
3. When was the last time you felt as though God was asking you to give up too much?
4. Read Hannah's story in 1 Samuel 1. Which of her feelings do you relate to most—her "bitterness of soul," her joy, her sacrifice, or her legacy? Why?
5. Does God always make up the difference from things He's asked us to give up? Why or why not?
6. Is God calling you to something new today? Are you willing to follow?

Recipe

More than a decade later, we are still making her pot stickers.

Lhamo was a Chinese student who lived in the girls' dorm during the years I worked at Auburn Adventist Academy, and she loved to cook. Once or twice every year, I would take her downtown to a giant Chinese grocery store, and we would buy cartfuls of ingredients whose labels I could not read. She would spend a full afternoon cooking and stirring and simmering things on my stove until an eight-course meal magically appeared on my table. "This is not food you will find at any Chinese restaurant," she announced. "This is how we actually cook in our homes, not what we cook for you Americans!" Scrambled eggs with tomatoes, ketchup, soy sauce, and sugar. Diced potatoes fried in peppers and black vinegar. Cucumber noodle salad and ginger broccoli I could eat bowlfuls of. But my favorite delicacy was always the pot stickers.

"Chinese women spend the afternoon together before a big meal, filling these," she explained. She showed us how to seal the edges and bend the ends just so. "My mother would *never* serve your pot stickers to guests, Mrs. Howell, they are so ugly!" she said with a laugh. "But don't worry—she usually never serves mine either." Some of my favorite Auburn afternoons were spent this way—sitting around a table with eight to ten girls, giggling and folding pot stickers, sneaking bites of the seasoned baked tofu from the mix, or gasping in desperation as yet another seam burst open. We sealed friendships on those days, not just wonton wrapper edges. And though Lhamo never had a single recipe for any of the food she made, I somehow sketched out a rough draft of what she used in which amounts—a pinch here and a scoop there. It's enough to duplicate the amazing dishes . . . almost. Because I still miss her presence at my table when I'm eating her food, and that was a main ingredient. Now, when my own guests—who do not notice my ugly novice folds—exclaim over how tasty the pot stickers are and ask for the recipe, I smile and state, "There isn't one. You'll just have to spend an afternoon with me."

The apricot pies are different. Those, I do have recipes for, and I'm happy to share. Grandma Palmer used to make an apricot pie every Thanksgiving just for me. Because I loved them so much, she started making them for Easter too, and Christmas, and even my birthday. When I went away to college, she made apricot pies to celebrate anytime I came home to visit. Then one sweltering August afternoon in her Arizona kitchen, she taught me how to make my own. While the apricots soaked, I listened to her stories of growing up on the farm and working during the war years. We stirred the bubbling mixture and added starch until it was thick enough. When we rolled the crust, she talked about her mother—a woman I never got to meet but who lives on in this pie crust recipe.

Grandma is old now—she turned ninety this year. That's too old to stand at the stove making apricot pies, or any pies. So now I have carried on the legacy, baking apricot pies for every Thanksgiving, Christmas, or Easter that the family gets together. Even when we don't get together, spread across the country as we are, I bake an apricot pie and serve it to the friends-like-family who join us for the occasion. I always carve a smiley-face steam vent in the top, the way Grandma always did for me. I always serve it on her china, and I always talk about my grandma.

This past Christmas we all came home to Arizona, and when she hobbled in the cabin's front door with her walker, she stopped first thing at the pie counter to exclaim over my pie. She promptly cut herself a piece to have as breakfast with her morning coffee, and she announced with pride, "Whoever made this apricot pie makes it *exactly* like I do." I beamed. No finer compliment could have been paid to me. I know I will always make apricot pie in her honor as long as I am able. And when I'm not, I'll pass the recipe down to another eager learner, with all the accompanying stories.

I love how recipes possess this magical way of keeping people close to us. Their power to transcend time and distance is remarkable to me: one taste of Mom's strawberry dip can have me standing in the old backyard on Scoville Avenue in my red spotted shorts during a summer party. A morning of Swedish pancakes takes me back to the tiny island shores where I was a student missionary with Miss Linda from Sweden. Chocolate mousse makes me think of giggling at midnight with my cousins in Palmdale. And tortellini soup will forever make me yearn for my sister's company over lunch. I've been told I am an amazing cook, but I can't help but be humbled by the fact that I most often simply stand on the shoulders of all the great cooks I've encountered. People come and go in our lives. They draw close and then move away. But keeping their recipes feels a little bit like keeping a part of them. For this reason, I have always been annoyed by people who don't share recipes. Not just because I can't make the food but also because they are denying me a chance of taking them with me when I go.

There are so many recipes for life that I wish I could pass on to my kids as easily as an index card transfer. I wish a surefire recipe for a relationship with Jesus existed. (Maybe it does?) I want to pass on the recipe for happiness and contentment. If I could somehow bottle up confidence and serve it to them, I certainly would. I'd also like to know the exact directions for growing the love of nature in a child, for nurturing the respect of life, and rubbing off the wonder of travel. I want the recipe for endurance during suffering and courage during fear. What if I could explain in six easy steps how to answer the quest for excellence, but not perfection? And if I could find the perfect recipe for forgiveness—dear God—I would first use it myself and then permanently paste it up on the refrigerator door and pass copies to everyone I know.

Sometimes I wonder: What life recipes are my children learning from me? Because some things are gleaned rather than taught, when we're busy sweeping up the egg shells and answering the veterinarian's phone call and we don't realize they're gleaning. But they are. They notice. I believe they notice my habits in exact proportion to how often they forget/ignore my directions. (Because I want to think there is a *reason* they "don't" hear me!) I know they learn lessons I never taught, because I sometimes suddenly see them mimicking my careful or careless ways. And that's downright terrifying.

But it's also pretty amazing. Because maybe . . . maybe if I'm so busy with the meals and the clothes and the house that I forget to talk often enough about the importance of prayer . . . maybe if they awake late in the night from a bad dream and find me alone with my Bible by the lamplight, it will be enough. I know I don't articulate the finer points of faith nearly as often as I repeat the mundane house rules, but they might still recognize that faith is the hinge that silently turns everything this family does, or doesn't do. I cannot give them the recipe for salvation, though I'd sell all I have to be able to. But my life's testimony may just give a pinch here and a scoop there, enough to inspire a taste for more than this world has to offer.

"Taste and see that the LORD is good," the psalmist invites (Psalm 34:8). I have questioned His goodness, unfortunately. More often than I'm proud of. But every time I truly "taste" the Lord in all His love and power and patience and faithfulness, I am amazed at just how incredibly good He is to me. God is *good*—so, so good! And when I really believe that God is good, I can safely filter any pain and sorrow that life has to offer. It's not a recipe. But it works. And I hope to pass it on whenever my children ask, but especially when they don't.

IN CASE YOU GET SIX MINUTES TO YOURSELF: STUDY GUIDE

1. What significant recipes have been passed down to you from friends and family?
2. Which significant life-recipes do you hope to pass on to your children?
3. What are the best ways for parents to pass on values to their children?
4. Read Psalm 34. What does verse 8 mean in the greater context of the whole psalm?
5. How can we "taste" the Lord? How can we pass on those "tastes" to others?
6. Which attribute of God's goodness are you personally needing to taste and experience today?

Father's Day

In some of my earliest memories, I am strapped into the little seat behind him on his bike, riding uphill to "the end of the street" on summer afternoons. I can still feel the wind in my hair as he'd push me on the rope swing that he hung from the old oak tree, still see the golden slant of the sun through its twisting branches. When my arms got long enough, Daddy would take me for motorcycle rides down dirt roads instead. The winter I was five, we rented a cabin in Big Bear, but the only thing I remember about that trip is how patiently he taught me to make pine-needle necklaces. How many beach days did we spend bending over tide pools as he showed me how to find sea anemones? He taught me how to dig for sand crabs on the shore, and then years later he taught me how to snorkel and even scuba dive. It wasn't often during my childhood that I woke up in the night, but I do recall waking up from a scary dream once, long after midnight, and finding him outside in the garage, working on the signs and clocks he sold to earn extra money for the family.

There are little things that stand out—like trips to Thrifty's for ice-cream cones, and the giant ice cubes he froze for us in old Cool Whip containers. Small moments, like first seeing the rings of Saturn or the cluster of the Pleiades through his telescope in the driveway and falling in love with the night sky. There are also big things, like the way he'd pile all the Primary-aged kids into the back of his pickup after church and take us hiking to the waterfall in the canyon—this is a big thing because it was somewhere in a curve of that canyon when I realized how much I loved the Sabbath. He gave that gift to me—a gift without a price tag. Big things, like the summers he gave up his only vacation time to take us trekking across the country in an old trailer, seeing the most magnificent sights America has to offer—Yosemite and Yellowstone, the Grand Canyon, Zion and the Tetons, the Salt Lake, Crater Lake, and more.

Some of the big moments were pivotal and life-altering, like the Christmas break I came home from college and announced I was giving up on theology and switching to social work instead, because the life of a woman in ministry would just be too hard. After a short silence, he said decisively, "Well, you are making a mistake. I think you were made for the ministry, and you would be wasting those gifts God made you with." I knew instantly that he was right. I changed back, followed a calling, and my life's work has testified to Dad's truth. There was also the day in the Texas restaurant when I complained about how I wished my new boyfriend had all of the things I wanted in a husband, qualities like my old friend Greg had, and Dad announced, "You have made it clear to me that you should be marrying Greg!" Once again, my heart recognized the truth the very second he said it. And I've been married to Greg for twelve years now.

Today, as a grown woman with my own family, I always smile to myself when I notice the ways Dad's influence still shows up in our lives. I think of him when my toddlers touch sea-anemone tentacles in tide pools and giggle. I freeze ice cubes in giant Tupperwares, we make pine-cone chains, and someone small always rides behind me in a bike seat. I spend afternoons pushing my kids on the rope swing he built in the forest when he last visited. We still hike on Sabbath afternoons. I find myself up long after midnight, writing for extra money. Since we live in Seattle and don't often have the chance to see the night sky, one afternoon I painted all the constellations on the ceiling of my boys' room. I want them to be able to find the Pleiades, Orion, Cygnus, and Vega, and fall in love with the night sky as I did. We go for ice cream in jammies before bedtime. We travel together any chance we get.

It's not that my dad was perfect and faultless or never made mistakes—he certainly had his share of bad times too. But sometimes we learn the greatest lessons from a person when they are at their worst. We learn how to fail gracefully, how to let go, how to say, "I'm sorry," and how to be faithful when it would be so much easier just to give up. In addition to memorizing Daddy's golden moments, I also studied him carefully during the hard times. I remember his shaking hand writing the tithe check with the last of the money in our family's account. I recall his Bible open on his lap when he was struggling and searching for life's answers. I can still quote the sayings he posted up in the garage when he lost his first business: "Never, never, NEVER give up," and "The rewards for those who persevere far exceed the pain that must precede the victory." Even in the hard times, the times that would look like failure to anyone else, he was actually teaching me how to fight, how to endure, how to cling to Jesus.

Once I asked Daddy what he'd like to have written on his gravestone someday, and he responded, "Only three words, Melissa: 'He was faithful.' "

I've often been told by counselors, teachers, and pastors that the way one views their earthly father will profoundly and dramatically affect how one views their heavenly Father. I suppose this is somewhat true. In fact, I have seen a lot of evidence supporting this idea throughout our years in ministry. If a person had a demanding and exacting father, they tend to believe that God is critical and expects perfection of them. The girls with absent or inattentive fathers struggle to believe that God loves and cares for them. People with enthusiastic, supportive fathers evidence the certainty that God is pleased with them. It's not an exact science, of course, but there seems to be some truth to it. Still, I never thought much of it until I returned to the journals.

I have written in prayer journals for almost twenty years now, since I was a teenager writing by porchlight in the backyard, pages flipping in the hot desert night wind. I seldom go back and reread those journals. However, during a trying time in the past year, I did find myself searching through pages spanning many eras of my life. The stories and the problems were as varied as the years, but I was surprised to discover one common, glaringly obvious theme threaded through each and every prayer I wrote to God: it was His name.

There are many, many names for God, of course. Some simply call Him "God" or prefer to address "Jesus" personally. Believers may call Him "Lord," while others prefer "Savior" or "Christ." Even the fancier names, like "Yahweh" and "El Shaddai," make appearances in people's prayer vocabulary from time to time. But those aren't the names that I use. Repeatedly, consistently, almost every single time I address the Divine in prayer, I call Him by one name only: "Father." Every prayer in every journal is addressed to the same person: my Father.

It's the closest name I could find for God. It's the name that tells me everything I need to know: that He values me, that He sees me, that He's faithful, and that He believes in me. "Father"—to me, the name speaks soundly of a legacy of love.

IN CASE YOU GET SIX MINUTES TO YOURSELF: STUDY GUIDE

1. What special memories do you have with your father, mother, or another important adult from your childhood?
2. What traditions from your childhood (or another time) would you like to create in your own family?
3. How was your own father like or unlike God? What view of God did you grow up with?
4. Have other important mentors of your life shaped the way you view God? How so?
5. If someone asked you to describe your heavenly Father, what would you say?
6. What is the most important thing you can teach your children about their heavenly Father?
7. What characteristics of a loving Father do you most need God to exhibit in your life today?

The Mother's Day Poem
I Never Got

My mother is the best because she always cuddles me when I'm sad!" the brown-bob-haired little girl in the pink skirt read. "She's as pretty as a butterfly, as sweet as a bunny, and as smart as a fox." Laughter gave way to thunderous applause as the little girl left the microphone and a boy in yellow approached.

It was the annual Mother's Day school picnic at the beach, and each child had prepared a special poem for his or her mother, complete with colorful borders and self-drawn portraits of their moms. The comments were funny, insightful, and inspiring.

"I love my mom because she makes the best pancakes."

"My mommy makes me clean my room even when I don't want to, because it's good for me."

"My favorite thing is when my mom takes me on bike rides, even when she's busy."

"Mommy always has time to play with me!"

With each passing child, I became more and more excited for my own son's turn at the mic. What would he say he loved about me? Would it be the game nights on the floor, the bedtime prayers, the silly voices, the evening hikes? How I bought him a puppy with all of my birthday money? How I help him comb his hair in the mornings? How does an eight-year-old boy notice my love for him? I couldn't wait to hear! Would he embarrass me? Make me cry? Of all the things I do, which ones mean the most to him? Anxiously, I scanned the line of adorable first- and second-graders, looking for my sweet boy's place in line.

That's when I realized he *wasn't* in line.

He wasn't leaning against the wall with the other kids in his class. He wasn't cueing up at the mic with his poem and artwork in hand. He wasn't even back in the hallway where I had left him. He wasn't anywhere.

Immediately I was on my feet, one twin on my hip, the other by the hand, stepping out of the row and scanning the small building for my boy. It didn't take me too long to find him, huddled on some chairs in the back, wringing his hands and crying. My husband, who was supposed to be manning the video camera for the presentation, knelt on the floor beside him instead, cell phone waving. I could see the frustration on Greg's face as he pointed at the phone and spoke in animated whispers to our firstborn. Before I reached them, however, his teacher caught me by the arm.

"Your son was absent yesterday when we worked on these," she whispered into my ear. "I told him he could just say a few things into the mic, but since he isn't prepared like the other kids, he won't. I've asked him three times now, and all three times he said he just doesn't want to." Suddenly, I understood. The trip to children's hospital for my daughter's surgery consultation yesterday. The missed hours of school. The other kids with their colored pictures, and him with none.

Realizing the situation, my husband had apparently jumped in with his cell phone at the last minute, trying to get our boy to make a short list of "nice things to say about mommy." But I already knew before I reached them that he wouldn't want to read from a cell phone if everyone else was reading from a colored paper. Our boy struggles with some pretty hefty things, you see—significant anxiety disorder, something which, I've learned, is passed on through families like brown hair or blue eyes. A gene we can't scold or cheer him out of. A battle he'll have to face and fight his whole life, simply because of his genetics.

I put a hand on my worried boy's leg as I approached him and wrapped my one free arm around his back as soon as I could. He buried his head in my neck, and I could hear the tears in his distraught little voice. "Mommy!" he whispered, "I just don't know what to say! I need to *think*! I don't have time! And I'll feel so silly if I read from a phone and none of the other kids do. I just don't know what to do!" he gushed into my ears.

Another child behind us read, "My mommy is the greatest gift of my very whole life," and the audience sighed together in one collective *"Awwwwww!"* And I realized—this was it.

This was my moment.

What kind of mother *would* I be today? Force my son to choke out a few endearing lines, drag him to the mic choking back tears, send him up there feeling conspicuous, just so that I could have my poem read? And for what—would that really be for me? Or would it be for the other women sitting in the crowd, who had spotted the commotion, the other women who would ask me later, "Why didn't *your* son read anything?" What did I need to know from him that I don't already know somewhere inside my heart?

It's true. I admit it—I wanted to hear that poem. I wanted everybody in the room to hear that poem because I am so darn proud of my son. But there was more, I realized with a start. *I* wanted to be like the other "kids" too (do we ever outgrow this feeling?). I wanted to have my great parenting moments recognized; I wanted to clap and cheer for my own darling child on the stage. But as I looked at that same darling child, clenching his fists in desperation, I already knew what mattered most.

"You don't have to read anything, sweetie," I whispered back to him.

"But Mommy, no! Then you will be sad! Then you will be the only mommy who didn't get a poem!" he hissed in earnest.

"It's OK," I insisted, "I don't need a poem. Just come back, come and sit by me."

"But won't you be sad?" he pressed me.

I took his rough hand, chapped and red from all the times he washes it in a day, when he starts to feel anxious about germs. I squeezed it tight. I looked him right in his fearful dark brown eyes, and said, "Sweetie, I'm just so happy to be here with you. I don't need a poem. I'm just happy to be your mommy and be here with my boy."

I know he believed me because the relief flooding his face was visible. "You just want to hear me sing, then? It's OK if I only sing songs with the other kids?"

"Absolutely!" I insisted. "That would be perfect."

We walked back to our row of chairs, hand in hand. He sat beside me nervously, while all the other kids in his class stepped up to the mic one by one and read their poems, and while all the other mothers in the class beamed and giggled and blushed, exploding with pride. Several times, he looked at me sideways, checking my face. Was I really OK? Did I lie to him? Was I terribly disappointed in him? So I smiled the most reassuring smile I could muster, for him. And as we sat there side by side, anxious mother and anxious son, listening to accolades of happy and playful mothers, I made a decision: I will write my own poem. I will write it for myself, right then, right there in that maroon plastic chair.

I love my mommy because she doesn't make me read poems up front when I haven't had enough time to prepare one, I began for him, in my head. But there was so much more . . . *I love my mommy because she understands me. She knows when too much is too much. She doesn't force me to be something I'm not. Sometimes she gives up things she was excited about, things she really wanted, to do what's best for me instead . . .*

Isn't this motherhood, really? Isn't *this*—this constant readjusting and always acquiescing to changes from what we had planned, what we had really wanted—isn't this motherhood? It's a thousand times a week of putting someone else before ourselves. It's adapting and letting go and changing again and again and again. It's the hopes and the dreams and the disappointments and the failures lined right up beside those moments of forever whispering, "It's OK, it's OK, it's OK." It's knowing that a child's little heart matters more than what anyone else thinks, what anyone else says, or what anyone else wants—including me.

I am actually as pretty as a butterfly (like, maybe one of those brown spotted ones?), and I'm certainly as smart as a fox, but no one in the room will ever know it because I am *mom* enough to see what my little boy needs. And that's my poem. That's *enough*. Happy Mother's Day to me.

But there was more poetry still to be written that day.

Later, after the singing and clapping were over and everyone was scrambling for the deviled eggs and brownies on the potluck table, another mother caught my arm in line. She is one of those gorgeous moms: long, thick black hair cascading over her trendy sweater, crystal-clear blue eyes set in a perfect porcelain face. "My daughter is so sad that your son is moving away," she told me. "Sometimes at night she even cries about him leaving!"

I felt surprised. "And do you know why she cries?" she continued. "I asked her once. Want to know what she said?"

I paused. Of course I wanted to know. "What?" I answered.

"She said that she's so sad your boy is leaving because he is the one person who always finds her on the playground when the other girls are being mean to her, or when someone's leaving her out. Your son—he finds her, and he makes sure she comes and plays with him. He makes sure she's always included. Thank you." She squeezed my arm.

"Thank *you*," I said, "for telling me. I had no idea."

She walked away and left me there near the taco salad, my heart swelling with pride and gratitude for my thoughtful, sweet son, for his kindness and his character. Her words were my poem that day—my *second* poem. And they were *enough*. More than enough, actually. Better than all the poems together.

After lunch I was down on the beach, reclining against a driftwood log with the other mothers, scanning the shoreline for our own. The kids played together in drift-wood forts, they scooped sand into buckets and threw giant rocks into the water for epic splashes.

Suddenly, I saw my boy approaching. His cheeks were red from running to the tide pools with his friends, his blonde hair sweaty in the hot afternoon sun. He strode confidently up the embankment to me, smelling of beach and boy and summertime, and held out his hand in front of my face. "Look at this, Mommy," he said and beamed. In his palm I saw a single white rock. "It's the whitest rock on the beach. I think it's the whitest rock I've ever seen in my life!" he exclaimed. "It's for you, Mommy. Keep it!" He placed the rock in my palm and smiled at me before running back to his post as captain of the fort.

He left his friends during a day at the beach . . . for me? To bring me the whitest rock on the beach. I rolled the rock in my hands, feeling its edges, feeling all our edges together—mothers and sons and daughters and families—all the sacrifice and all the pain and all the joy. I slipped the rock into my pocket. I will keep it. It was my poem that day—my *third* poem. And it is *enough*.

We are enough.

IN CASE YOU GET SIX MINUTES TO YOURSELF: STUDY GUIDE

1. What are your favorite types of things to receive for Mother's Day?
2. When was the last time you had to choose between enjoying something you wanted and doing what your child needed?
3. If someone were to compliment your child, what is the greatest compliment they could give you?
4. Does God struggle between doing what He wants and giving us what we need? Or are they one and the same to Him?
5. As God's child, when was the last time you refused to do something or found yourself crippled by fear? How do you think He responded to you?
6. How can you know the difference between things that He accepts and things He wants you to change?
7. What are the things you need your heavenly Father to simply know, understand, and accept about you today?

Camera Roll

Currently I have 8,236 photos on the camera roll of my iPhone. Before you judge me for how ridiculous this is (at which point I would agree with you), let me just tell you about some of them first.

Photo number 346 is of my shoes filled with miniature violet-and-white May windflowers, with my bare feet off in the corner of the picnic blanket. My two sons collected the flowers for me—collected so many, in fact, that I couldn't even hold them anymore, so I filled up my shoes. That first sunny day of the season released us from the bonds of the house and sent us out to bask on blankets under brilliant blue skies. I felt so alive and happy I could burst. We played Frisbee and collected sticks for sword fighting and snacked on string cheese. I loved that day! I'm keeping that picture.

Photo number 2,116 features my yellow lab, Summer, running at full ear-flapping speed down a forest trail with my kids behind her, all heading straight for me. It was the day we found out she had stage 3 terminal cancer. We were told we would lose her in a matter of months, and we could think of nothing else to do but take her to the places she loved the most. She tore through the trees that day and leaped through the mud, blissfully oblivious of what lurked inside her. I didn't know it at the time, but it would be her last trip to those woods. We lost her sooner than I had anticipated. And while I can't exactly say I love that picture or that it makes me very happy—I'm still keeping it.

Somewhere around number 3,000, my twins came into the world and thereafter dominated the roll for the next thousand shots or so—babies through Plexiglas hooked up to wires, babies in car seats coming home, babies in arms, babies snuggling, babies meeting my mommy and my sister.

Photo number 4,872 is my old high-school flame and first love. I screen-captured the photo off his Facebook account. Don't tell him this—but I keep it precisely because every time I scroll past it, I take a moment to thank the good Lord that I did *not* marry him.

Photo number 6,631 boasts all four of my adorable babies in the pumpkin patch on a crisp autumn day's end.

Photo number 7,052—my sister and me with my ninety-one-year-old grandpa, wearing his WWII veteran hat, on the day my grandma lived through a heart attack. It makes me think of survival of many types—from sinking ships in the waters of the Pacific to helicopter airlifts that arrived in just enough time.

Photo number 1,925 shows my kids under a fireworks-lit sky on the Fourth of July, faces aglow, bare feet dirty on the neighborhood street.

Priceless memories. Moments captured. Lessons and laughter frozen in time. This camera roll is the photojournalism of my life over the past two years, of every single moment that I thought was somehow significant and photo-worthy. When you scroll through it quickly, as I often do, you can easily get a sense of what this particular season of life and motherhood has looked like for me.

But there are other photos too. Photos that aren't on any camera roll anywhere. Snapshots in time captured only by my memory's eye. Like the night I sat on the kitchen floor covered in the blood that wouldn't stop oozing from my toddler's sliced hand. (It was only later that I saw the bloody, jagged edge of the tin can he had fished out of the trash when my back was turned.) Nobody took a picture of me that night as I held his hand above his head and applied pressure on the cut for more than an hour, whispering prayers that the bleeding would just stop. No one snapped the shot, but that picture is etched in my mind forever.

There also isn't a picture of me pacing the halls at Children's Hospital, cradling my baby girl just before they took her into surgery. But I looked down at her face when we stopped beside the fish tank, and I don't think I'll ever forget how beautiful she looked to me just then.

There are no pictures of me cleaning up vomit at four o'clock in the morning, none of me changing poopy diapers for the twelfth time in one day, and none at all of me loading the dishwasher or sweeping crumbs off the floor or doing laundry—though there really should be pictures of them somewhere, because I do all of those maybe fifty-seven times each and every single day.

Tonight I was wondering which camera roll captures motherhood better: the one on my phone or the one in my memory. My phone showcases mostly posed, still moments—when everyone was smiling or being cute. But the bulk of motherhood is not posed. Can I also say that the bulk of motherhood is not even cute? Stumbling down the hall at four in the morning toward screaming babies is not cute. Mountains of dirty socks and pee-soaked bed sheets are not cute. The way my pre-pregnancy jeans fit? Absolutely, definitely not anything close to cute. And this list could go on and on and on—filled with so many annoyances and disgusting tasks of motherhood that are anything but happy and cute.

Mentally scrolling through my other unseen "camera roll," I am reminded of a poem my good friend Katie wrote as a wedding gift for my husband and me. The poem compared marriage to a stained-glass window—so many happy, shining, colorful moments, and yet between them can be found such harsh, rough darkness. The poem ended by posing the question, "What is more important in stained glass—bright light beaming through brilliant colors, or dark mortar melding, welding all into one?"

I am asking myself the same question about motherhood. Which matters more—the happy times or the rest of the time? When our children grow up and we sit around "remembering when," of course we will want to recall the shining moments, the bright times, the trips to the beach and holiday parties and summer nights camping under the stars. But right now, in the thick of motherhood, I guess I'm struck tonight by the idea that maybe the dark times matter more, the off-camera times that no one can or will see but God. I think that the sleepless night I spent by the bedside of my feverish son whispered more of an "I love you" than a dozen beach walks ever could have. My babies don't care too much about our Christmas card photos, but they certainly do notice when their cries go unanswered. Dishes and laundry and grocery shopping don't create any family memories, but they keep us functioning; they keep us fed and hold us together. The endless cycle of these tasks can make my life feel so futile and meaningless, and yet—they are the black mortar, melding, holding the happy times together. The one thousand invisible tasks that I do behind the scenes for my children give them the luxury of enjoying their childhood as worry-free as the world will possibly allow.

So much of my Christian walk has followed this same camera roll, stained-glass pattern. There have been shining moments, for sure—mountaintop experiences where I saw the hand of God, felt the Lord's unmistakable leading, or experienced that intoxicating intimacy of God's Spirit. Oh, how I loved those times! They are my highlights, snapshots of glory to treasure until we see Him face to face. But honestly, I don't have as many of them as I'd like. What I have a lot more of are ordinary days. Times of drudgery. So many bland, habitual times—going to church week after week, blessing the food and family devotions, fighting for just a little time to daily talk with God: the dishes and laundry of the Christian life. They certainly don't feel like much at all, in the same way that motherhood's menial tasks don't feel significant or important in the slightest. But I have come to believe that these humble habits are the mortar of my faith. I won't be doing any foundational building of my faith during a crisis, because I'll likely be barely holding on at all during that time. But I will be holding on regardless, precisely because I took the time to strengthen my faith before the challenge came.

In both Christianity and motherhood, I so much prefer the happy times. I like the camera-roll-worthy moments of joy and wonder and passion so much better. I endure all the work and mess and chaos and hassle because I have to. I force myself through those times in hopes that laughter and smiles and cuddles will be around the next corner. I force myself through heartbreak or silence from God because I have learned to hope that blessings will be around the next corner too. And in both of these areas of life—motherhood and faith—I know that true growth happens when we are down on our knees doing the hard work.

I'm humbled by the fact that God sees all these pictures. But more, by the fact that He is my Companion through them all. I take the pictures because I'm afraid of forgetting—I want to remember! He never forgets. Anything. He remembers my moments. He can bring them back to me just as I need them, even when I have forgotten. He sees all my moments and knows how to piece them together into something beautiful: a mosaic of motherhood that His light is ever shining through.

IN CASE YOU GET SIX MINUTES TO YOURSELF: STUDY GUIDE

1. What are some of your favorite moments and memories from your motherhood years? Do you have pictures of these times?
2. What are some of your worst ones? Would you even want pictures of these times?
3. What are the mountaintop experiences in your walk with Jesus? The valleys?
4. During which times—happy or sad—do you see more growth happening?
5. How can you harvest the joy from good times and use it to propel yourself through hard times?
6. Do you find yourself in light times or dark times today? In which areas do you need God's light to shine through?

Stay-at-Home Extrovert

How many times in a day can a person think the phrase "I'm so lonely" without actually going crazy?

I am a stay-at-home mommy. And I am an extrovert. Which makes me a stay-at-home extrovert, and this is an extremely difficult combination.

There are a lot of positives to being an extroverted mommy, for sure. People say that it seems like my family is always having fun. I'm good at creating adventure and excitement in ordinary, every-day moments. I'm driven to make sure our lives are full of friends. We surround ourselves with lots of people and engage in many outside activities. We throw epic parties as often as we can. Our family is always going somewhere, doing something, always searching for the next exciting thing. Being extroverted can be a huge asset in motherhood. But it can be an extremely difficult obstacle as well.

Being extroverted doesn't just mean that I'm outgoing or talkative or the life of the party—though I can be those things. Introverts can be talkative and outgoing too; in fact, many of them are. The extrovert/introvert difference is in where a person gets their energy from. Introverts become energized by being alone, having quiet space and time to think. Extroverts receive energy from being with other people. One can decipher which is truest about themselves by considering what drains them: if being around too many people for too long drains you, then you are an introvert. If being alone for too many hours of the day drains you, then you are an extrovert.

Hence, staying at home with my children all day is something I find very draining. And by the way, I should add that children don't necessarily count as "people" in the discussion of where one gets energy from. Though they can fill us or drain us, and often do both, the level of conversation capability is far from being equally met. For example—I feel really great and "filled up" after talking to a group full of other women for an hour. But I don't get that same result from talking to my children about Batman, poop, the Force, what's for dinner, don't touch that, and where their coats disappeared to.

What I find most inconvenient about this personality/life choice clash is that I am so dependent on other people. I cannot fill myself up—I just can't. I need people, and that's a fact. I cannot be my fullest self without people, and that means I can't be the fullest mommy to my children, either. So all of us suffer if I don't get to connect with someone. I start to get empty and depressed, or just kind of listless, and I do that wandering-aimlessly-around-the-house thing. But many days, it's hard to find another mommy who has time to pack up her children and drag them over to my house even for just a thirty-minute chat. It's hard to pack up my own four kids in the dead of winter and just hang out in a grocery store or a shopping mall so I can feel like I'm around other people—that doesn't really cut it either. The bottom line is that I can function best when I've had a certain amount of people time every single day, and that's just not always possible.

So what am I supposed to do? I've asked for advice from lots of other moms. My sister Heather says I just need to get out of the house once every single day. Janella admits that she relies on her husband for conversation at the end of the day, when friends can't be contacted. Lizzie advises me to create a playdate schedule. Lora related that she had to learn to enjoy her own company—and I'm still mulling over that one. Alicia insists I need to go back to work because staying at home is making me depressed. Missy encouraged me to become involved in a local MOPS group in town. My mother thinks I should call one person every day (and I know she meant herself when she said that, haha). Christi's idea was to write about it. (I am!) And Angela insists that all I need to do is move next door to her (although she's an introvert—she'd throw me out after an hour). But what is the real answer? What are we extroverts with limited budgets, busy friends, and numerous children supposed to do?

Is it possible for God to be my company? Can He take the place of my friends, can conversation with Him fulfill the social needs my personality craves? I don't know. I trust that every need we have can somehow be met in Him. But I also believe that He created us to live in community. I've asked Him to take away my loneliness. I've prayed that I could find a way for my children to fill my friendship needs. I've questioned whether the loneliness would disappear if I spent more time with God. And I've wrestled for many years over whether I truly should be a stay-at-home mommy, though it is what I want with all my heart. Should I change the dreams and goals I hold for motherhood just because my personality struggles? I don't think so. At least, I'm not ready to do that yet.

Sometimes I think about the loneliest people in the Bible—Elijah isolated in the wilderness for years, being fed by ravens. Who did he talk to? Jeremiah in his misery, writing Lamentations, hating his life. Cain banished from his family, who were literally the only people on earth at that time. The demon-possessed man among the pigs. John stranded on Patmos. Or David alone in the fields tending his sheep and playing his harp through the empty hours.

It is David's story in particular that catches me. I think he was an extrovert—well, I assume that, from reading his stories and psalms—but I don't know for sure. Anyhow, when we meet David as a ruddy, handsome boy, youngest of all his brothers, there is already something remarkable about him, for the Lord directs Samuel to anoint him as the future king of Israel. The reason God gives for this surprising choice is that "the LORD does not look at the things people look at. People look at the outward appearance, but the LORD looks at the heart" (1 Samuel 16:7). Which tells me that there was something special about David's heart—something unusual, something worthy of becoming a king—because no outward beauty could ever recommend a heart to God. (Maybe we should try to see people the same way?)

Later on, we see David soothe the evil spirits out of Saul with his harp, even under occasions of death threats. Next we find David on the battlefield without armor, fighting a giant with a piece of leather and some rocks. David was the only man in all of Israel with courage enough to confront the Philistine. After this victory, he goes on to win many more battles and finally to become king over all Israel, truly a "man after [God's] own heart" (Acts 13:22).

What comprised the secret to all his success? One historical commentator says,

> The Lord had chosen David, and was preparing him, in his solitary life with his flocks, for the work He designed to commit to his trust in after years. . . . David had proved himself brave and faithful in the humble office of a shepherd, and now God had chosen him to be captain of His people. . . . Daily revelations of the character and majesty of his Creator filled the young poet's heart with adoration and rejoicing. . . . He was daily coming into a more intimate communion with God. His mind was constantly penetrating into new depths for fresh themes to inspire his song. . . .
>
> Who can measure the results of those years of toil and wandering among the lonely hills? The communion with nature and with God, the care of his flocks, the perils and deliverances, the griefs and joys, of his lowly lot were not only to mold the character of David and to influence his future life, but through the psalms of Israel's sweet singer they were in all coming ages to kindle love and faith in the hearts of God's people.*

I'm not sure what the secret to success is as a stay-at-home extrovert, but I do know that if the great King David's strength foundation came from his quiet days tending sheep and talking with the Lord, maybe mine can too. Here I am myself, tending sheep, guiding little ones. I am lonely often, it is true. But that doesn't mean God can't still be using these years for good in spite of my loneliness. If loneliness

---

* Ellen G. White, *Patriarchs and Prophets* (Mountain View, CA: Pacific Press®, 1958), 637–642.

draws me to seek Him more, all the better. If He's teaching me something here, though I am not yet aware of it, one day I will look back on it and be grateful. David's quiet days prepared him for all that awaited him in his future. I don't know what awaits me in my future. So for now, I'll keep chasing after playdates and phone calls, God's company, and my own little sheep.

IN CASE YOU GET SIX MINUTES TO YOURSELF: STUDY GUIDE

1. Are you an extrovert or an introvert? Where do you get your energy from?
2. What are the particular frustrations and challenges of having this personality type in motherhood? What are the blessings and benefits?
3. Why is motherhood sometimes so lonely, whether one works or stays at home?
4. Is it possible for God to meet our social needs? Why or why not?
5. Read the story of David's early years in 1 Samuel 16–18, and read the chapter on David's boyhood years in *Patriarch and Prophets,* chapter 62. What can you learn about motherhood from the life of David?
6. What things in the future might motherhood be preparing you for? How have you grown? How do you still need to grow?

Thanksgiving Redo

It's after midnight now, and Thanksgiving is officially over. I'm sitting in my dark living room by the light of one solitary lamp, relaxing for the very first time today. The only sounds are the hum of the dishwasher and the jingling bell on the cat's collar as she eats—out of hiding for the first time all day. The conclusion my exhausted mind keeps coming to is that this was not much of a Thanksgiving for me. Not much of a day of thanks, that is.

I spent most of the day cooking and cleaning. And then cooking more, and then cleaning up that, and cooking, and setting tables, clearing tables, and cleaning some more. So much preparation and money and time went into this day, but the day itself was not much fun at all—it held pockets of fun. But it didn't resemble Thanksgiving to me—this is supposed to be a day to stop, reflect, mark time. We remember the first brave settlers in our land, the generous natives. We realize anew all that we have to be thankful for—food, family, safety, home, health, blessings—and then we try to enjoy those things. Or at least, I think that's the idea.

But that's not how I spent my day at all. I didn't reflect on blessings or meditate on my life in thankfulness. I barely even gave a minute's notice to the old Thanksgiving story. Since I didn't set my mind on the things one ought to be thinking about on Thanksgiving, maybe you are wondering what I did think about. Well, I'll tell you.

I woke up thinking about preparing the turkey . . . *How much butter will I need for the turkey rub? I have fresh sage and thyme, but do I have enough fresh rosemary? There is turkey skin under my fingernails; I need to take a shower. Both babies are crying—better feed them first. Better feed the older boys too. Shower. Get dressed—no, this is not a good Thanksgiving outfit. Get dressed again—oh wow, this doesn't fit me anymore. Get dressed again—perfect, I look nice, good colors, this sweater is really warm but maybe it's worth it, it will be OK. Begin the long day of cooking. Cutting, stirring, stuffing, shuffling dishes around in the oven to make them all fit. Laying out appetizer trays, trying to get a few bites of it before it disappears. When will the turkey be done? Is it getting too dry? Which casserole dish will I prepare next? Better run the dishwasher. My word, this sweater is getting hot. How am I going to lay this meal out on the counter? I know you're hungry, I'm working on it! Is everything going to be ready at once? Is it one thousand degrees in here, or is it just my sweater? Oh no, some dishes are getting cold already! Who is supposed to be cutting the turkey? I have watched my aunt make that gravy all my life, how is it that at this moment I can't think how to make it? I better set the table—wait, have I unpacked Grandma's good china or is it still in a box somewhere? I feel like a boiling anaconda is wrapped around my neck—I hate this sweater. We are out of clean forks again. Time to eat! Which of these foods will the babies not choke on? Is there even room on my plate to sample all eleven dishes? Wow, this food is so amazing. I love to eat! I especially love the taste of—wait—why is she smearing cranberry Jell-O all over her forehead? Is that handfuls of mashed potatoes he threw on the floor? No, you cannot have pie if you only eat three and a half bites of your dinner! Oh, pie—should I start warming them? What do you mean, you don't like turkey? Hold on—is everyone done eating already? I just started. It looks like a bomb went off in my kitchen. Oh, this pie is so-o-o-o-o amazing. I love Thanksgiving. I'm taking this sweater off right now.*

I've heard I'm not the only woman who possesses this annoying talent of turning a wonderful holiday celebration into an OCD, stress-to-the-max nightmare. From what I understand, it's fairly common to get so lost in the details of an event that we miss the point entirely. Let's be honest—there really *are* a *lot* of things we have to think about even on a normal day. But add a normal day's routine to the frenzy of a holiday, and you've just concocted a pretty overwhelming mix for a mommy. It's no wonder that there isn't much space left in our heads to think about the things that truly matter.

The day wasn't a total loss. There were several special moments squeezed in between the hectic ones. I did notice them. I just wish I had taken more time to focus on them, to remain in them, instead of hurrying myself back to the baking.

Here are the things I wish I had spent time thinking about:

My one-year-old twin boy sat outside the glass door as I showered, waiting for me. He was holding my pajama shirt all wrapped up in a ball—I assume because it smelled like me and that brought him comfort. He giggled as he played with the clips and bobby pins and lotions in my bathroom drawers.

In the middle of the cooking chaos, my four-year-old came bouncing into the kitchen exclaiming, "Mommy, look!" He held out a piece of scrap wood with one single nail pounded into it. The wood had been entirely colored in scribbly red marker. He proudly explained to me in excitement that all the red stuff is lava and the nail is a gun, and the gun shoots bullets. The gun can turn into a man too. The man can jump out of the lava and find his home but the lava is getting closer. There is one black spot in the wood and that is where all the lava came from. Did I even respond to this creative explanation at all? Did I praise him for his ingenuity? I should have. I hope I did.

At some point between the dinner cleanup and the mad dash to the pies, my six-year-old son asked me to come and play hide-and-seek with him. I did have enough sense to recognize that moments when he asks me to play appear fewer and fewer these days, so I descended the stairs and went to find him and the other kids. The telltale giggles came from my linen closet. I opened it up to find one child on every single shelf. Towels cascading down everywhere. "Good hiding place," I managed, "but now I expect all these towels to be folded up and put away." I went back upstairs to fuss over something. I wish I had stayed to play. I wish I had taken a picture of the linen closet with a snickering, happy kid on every shelf.

Our best friends joined our relatives for the holiday. We all took a moment to watch the sun setting fiery orange and pink over the cascades and the Puget Sound, leaning over the deck railing with warm mugs of cider in hand. We took the dog for a walk around the dark neighborhood and talked about motherhood challenges.

My handsome husband enjoyed his yearly plate of five slices of pie.

When everyone finally went to bed and the house was silent and dark, I let myself outside and looked up into the chilly night air at a million stars. (I didn't even have my darn sweater then, but maybe I finally would have appreciated it.) How blessed I am, I realized—my beautiful children, this home in the woods we live in! Look at all the food we were able to buy. Could I ever count all our blessings? They seem more numerous than the stars above. I took a moment right then and there, for the first time all day, to genuinely thank God for all the pleasures we enjoy.

If I could have a redo on this Thanksgiving, these are the things I would make the day about instead. We don't get redos, though. Just chances to live differently next time.

IN CASE YOU GET SIX MINUTES TO YOURSELF: STUDY GUIDE

1. How do you tend to behave during the holidays? What do you focus on?
2. What are some of your favorite holiday memories with your children?
3. How different did the day feel from the perspective of thankfulness, rather than hurriedness? Is it possible to live only in thankfulness? How?
4. What are some of the things you are the most thankful for in life?
5. Reviewing your own day today, if you could do it over again, what things would you change?

An Open Letter to the Proverbs 31 Woman

Hello, pure and perfect lady of matchless, unmarred character. It's time you and I had a little heart-to-heart chat.

See, there's this crowning tribute written about you in the very last chapter of Proverbs, and it paints you as an immaculate ideal. Which makes a whole lot of us feel guilty and lacking in comparison. You've set impossible, unattainable standards for flawed women everywhere, and that's not really very nice. Or fair. Nor will it make you many friends, mind you, being so superior and all. I mean, you're kind of like the biblical equivalent of the most popular girl in school, the valedictorian of the class, the mom who buys/grows only organic food, the woman who runs her own three businesses, and the wife who comes to every party looking like a million bucks. And while we all admire those people, we don't necessarily "like" them, if you know what I mean. Well, actually, in all your virtue and holiness, you probably *don't* know what I mean, so, please, allow me to explain.

Let's just jump right in with your opening introduction: "A wife of noble character who can find? She is worth far more than rubies" (verse 10). So, first of all, almost *all* of us struggle with feeling worthless at some time or another. But here you are, being worth more than *rubies,* for crying out loud. Instead of tagging and bragging about your worth, maybe you should share some secrets with us on how to find our worth in the midst of overachievers like you who only threaten it. Second—your noble character. I want to have a noble character. I honestly strive and seek to have a noble character. But there's still so much I struggle with, so many ways I fail, so many times I act less than noble. I guess you wouldn't know anything about that.

Moving on: "Her husband has full confidence in her and lacks nothing of value. She brings him good, not harm, all the days of her life" (verses 11, 12). It is one of the deepest desires of my heart to give my husband the gift of full confidence in me. How hard we lesser women try to be good wives, to be faithful and true. We want our husbands to know they can trust us to guard our hearts (and bodies) from the lure of other handsome faces. We try to make sure that his reputation will be completely safe on our lips, in all conversations. We also endeavor to boost his confidence in us as mothers, cooks, caretakers, and homemakers. But I don't think a single one of us (except you) could say that our husbands lack nothing of value. Listen, lady— we are all lacking something! Have you really never brought your husband harm? Not even for *one* of the days of your life? I'd like to think I heal him far more than I harm him, but isn't some harm inevitable? Aren't we human? Aren't *you*?

"She selects wool and flax and works with eager hands. She is like the merchant ships, bringing her food from afar" (verses 13, 14). Girlfriend—I wouldn't even know the difference between wool and flax if I were wrapped in it, for real. Do you particularly enjoy wool and flax? Are they your favorite hobbies? Because who among us works with eager hands, unless we're working on something we love and enjoy? My hands have never once tingled with eagerness to scour the oven, never once scrubbed poop stains out of onesies with eager glee. Maybe your wool and flax never get poop stained? And what's this bit about the merchant ships, flax lady—my food comes from the closest, cheapest sources, definitely not from "afar." (The 7.3 billion plastic "Made in China" toys in my house—now they all come from afar—granted. But that's different.)

"She gets up while it is still night . . ." (verse 15). Now that's just going too far. If someone out there didn't hate you before, they sure do hate you now. Give us a break, goddess! *Who* in their *right mind* gets up while it is still night, unless they *have to*? Admittedly, I've gotten up while it was still night many times. However, that was to nurse babies, or to comfort crying kids and clean up vomit, or to drive to my job at an ungodly hour. So, to do this on purpose? By choice? No. I'm not even going to applaud you for this—this is just wrong. This is not a virtue: this is sad for you. Sleep is a virtue, sleep is a treasure, sleep is what's worth more than rubies! You've definitely got this part backwards. See? I knew you had faults.

"She provides food for her family and portions for her female servants" (verse 15). OK, so now I'm starting to see why you get to twiddle your fingers in flax all day— you have servants! Glory be! Well, news flash: I don't have servants. And I never will. I don't know what those servant girls actually do for you, since it sounds like you still do all the cooking. (You're a poor delegator? *Yessss,* another defect, check!) Oh I try to provide food for my family too, but it's crazy-hard on a tight single budget with bottomless boy tummies to fill. Some days the pantry gets pretty bare. If I had servants, they would end up eating ramen and rice like the rest of us, until the paycheck came through.

But that must be why you facilitated this next part: "She considers a field and buys it; out of her earnings she plants a vineyard" (verse 16). Clever girl. Earning and investing! I'd totally love to invest, if I had anything left to invest. I've considered a used car, and bought it. Never mind about how that turned out. I consider buying other things too, you know: books and boots and clothes, manicures and massages and trips to Paris. Some of us can't buy everything we want, though. Also, it sounds like your yard is clearly larger than mine. Forget a vineyard—I just want to plant three rosebushes. Maybe I can use a corner of your field?

"She sets about her work vigorously; her arms are strong for her tasks" (verse 17). You know—this is inspiring, it really is. I'd like to be known as a vigorous worker, full of passion, purpose, and energy. That would be awesome. And strong arms—oh, I do covet those nice sculpted biceps that gym women have. But I carry two twenty-five-pound toddlers around all day, and it doesn't seem to help. How many reps would that equal, anyways? I don't know, but I digress. I think this means you are motivated, intentional, and capable. I'd love to cultivate all of those qualities. But I don't think sitting here comparing myself to you is really going to help me do that.

"She sees that her trading is profitable, and her lamp does not go out at night" (verse 18). Well *now* we have some similarities, supermom! My lamp doesn't go out at night either . . . usually because I'm up finishing something I didn't accomplish all day, or because I just fell dead asleep with the lamp still on. But, hey. This still puts me in league with you, does it not? Oh, I think it does. If you're doubtful, I'll point out that my trading is profitable too—you wouldn't believe how much money I've made on Craigslist and eBay! No, no, don't ask where it's gone . . . no, I didn't buy a vineyard; I said don't ask!

"In her hand she holds the distaff and grasps the spindle with her fingers" (verse 19). You know how sometimes your kids say something, and you retort, "That's not even worth an answer"? Yeah. This is one of those times. Distaff and spindle? I'll see your distaff and spindle for my microwave and iPhone. What now? Oh, you don't know what I'm talking about? Huh. That feels bad, doesn't it? Yeah. OK, wait, I just Googled (didn't know about that either, did you?) the words *distaff* and *spindle,* and I cannot believe it; this is about flax. Again. You need to lay off the flax, sister su-preme. I think you're a teensy bit obsessed.

"She opens her arms to the poor and extends her hands to the needy" (verse 20). This is important. This matters. Way to go! I always want to be aware of the needs of those less fortunate than I am. But not just aware. I hope to find practical ways to provide help. It's difficult with a house of small children already to care for, though. But I'd like to teach them by example that caring for the needy is what Jesus asks us to do. And it's awesome, it feels great. I want them to experience that. This needs to find a place in my already overcrowded schedule.

"When it snows, she has no fear for her household; for all of them are clothed in scarlet" (verse 21). We generally are clothed in Columbia when it snows, but hey. I like how you are prepared for the worst here—that's cool. It's good to think about those things. But it's not cool to show off about them, OK?

"She makes coverings for her bed; she is clothed in fine linen and purple" (verse 22). We wash the sheets for our beds. Some of us might quilt (not me), but probably not with flax or fine linen.

"Her husband is respected at the city gate, where he takes his seat among the elders of the land" (verse 23). I'm confused—is this about you, or him? Is it showing that, among all your other attributes, you also have impeccable choice in men? Or is he respected because of you—is that even possible? Can a woman cause her husband to gain respect? Oh. Maybe so. I'll think about that one.

"She makes linen garments and sells them, and supplies the merchants with sashes" (verse 24). *Sigh.* What do I make? What do I contribute to society? Am I even contributing healthy, happy kids? Some days I don't know, some days I feel like I'm doing it all wrong. Thanks for listening.

"She is clothed with strength and dignity; she can laugh at the days to come" (verse 25). I've been trying to avoid saying this, but I can't hide it any longer: I really do admire a whole lot of things about you. Particularly this one. What qualities do I wear like wardrobes? Distractedness, impatience, irritability. I think strength is in my closet somewhere; actually, I know it is, because there have been very naked days when that's all I've had to wear. Dignity, well, that's close to pride, and the line is so fine I just might step over it. Seriously though, strength and dignity—much better than scarlet, fine linen, and purple. Better than rubies, even, if I dare say so. And the fact that you can laugh at the days to come means you're not stressed about the future. How I wish I could say the same. There's a lot about the future that stresses me out regularly.

"She speaks with wisdom, and faithful instruction is on her tongue. She watches over the affairs of her household and does not eat the bread of idleness. Her children arise and call her blessed; her husband also, and he praises her" (verses 26–28). I think I eat loaves and loaves of that bread. Even though I am also constantly running all day . . . I know, it doesn't make sense to me either. But it sounds like you are a great mom and wife. You've got the wisdom to teach your kids valuable life lessons. Almost daily, I beg God for wisdom to train my children well. I hope He's giving it to me. I don't always see the signs of it. Your husband cheers for you. And your kids—they even like you. They call you blessed. My kids call me a whole lot of things (most not worthy of writing), but not *blessed*. I think if I got to choose, though, I'd like for them to call me love giver, hug expert, joy infuser. "Blessed" is cool too, though. No, really.

"Many women do noble things, but you surpass them all" (verse 29). I'm sorry, but honestly? This is why people don't like you. Skillful, spotless, superb surpasser. That's you. And *none* of us.

"Charm is deceptive, and beauty is fleeting; but a woman who fears the LORD is to be praised" (verse 30). In the end, none of your scarlet-wearing, vineyard-planting, flax-weaving ways are going to matter—hate to break it to you. What matters *most*, and this means *above all,* is the fear and honor of the Lord. We lean on our toolboxes of charms far too often. Every day, that mirror affirms how fleeting beauty truly is. But the fear of the Lord—that's something that can't be taken away, that's something worth working for. You've got this figured out.

"Honor her for all that her hands have done, and let her works bring her praise at the city gate" (verse 31). I don't know what my reward will be someday for all the senseless days and hours I have spent cooped up in this house. But I know what my reward is now. It's them—my babies—the reason I am here. I could never have done anything worthy of earning their sweet love, but it's mine anyway. I marvel. And whatever reward I might receive in heaven won't be by my earnings at all. It will be on the merit and mercy of Jesus Christ. Compared to Him, even *you* don't measure up. And that's saying a whole lot.

Whew. I think we're finally finished with you.

To be fair, I know you don't actually exist. (But isn't it equally as easy to despise a fairy tale?) You never lived. You were a made-up example, a standard, the height of what a young man should search for in a woman. I know that this little bit about you in Scripture was likely written by King Solomon, whose mother, Bathsheba, probably taught it to him as a song. That alone is a somber realization, when we consider all that Bathsheba saw and lived through, and later all the less-than-worthy wives that Solomon ended up with. Maybe she spotted this tendency in him early on. (Don't we see sin sneaking up in our sweet ones?) Maybe she tried to inoculate him against it by writing about you. When I think of the measures I'd like my own three sons to use when choosing a wife, I suddenly become quite fond of excellent, indefectible you.

What I like even more, though, is that scholars believe this song about you is arranged in the same style as hymns that were sung to valiant warriors. This would have been done in order to compare you as equal to a warrior. To think of you, or any woman, or any mother, as a warrior? Wow. That really works for me. That is absolutely, exactly what we are. How many silly and serious battles do we daily fight? How many wounds have we sustained, on our bodies and our hearts? Wouldn't every last one of us die willingly for just one of our precious children? Yes, without hesitation, we would. We are warriors. The fights we fight in our homes, jobs, schools, and vineyards (whatever the case may be) are significant and powerful. We don't have to be perfect to be warriors. And though it seems like we are just mediocre moms who don't particularly excel at anything excellent or praiseworthy (in contrast to you), we are all still soldiers for God on the battlefields of our children's minds and characters.

> The mother seldom appreciates her own work and frequently sets so low an estimate upon her labor that she regards it as domestic drudgery. She goes through the same round day after day, week after week, with no special

marked results. She cannot tell at the close of the day the many little things she has accomplished. . . . She feels that she has done nothing worth mentioning. . . .

Could the veil be withdrawn and father and mother see as God sees the work of the day, they would be astonished at the heavenly revelation. . . . The mother has been dealing with developing minds and characters, working not only for time, but for *eternity*.*

What about those times when you and I can't be warriors? In those times when we fall, when we're spent and depleted, or when we just can't stand in the gap for our children—it's OK. There is still another: "The Lord is a warrior; the Lord is his name" (Exodus 15:3). "The Lord, strong and mighty; the Lord, invincible in battle" (Psalm 24:8, NLT).

Thanks for your time today, Proverbs 31 warrior woman. You're all right. We all are.

IN CASE YOU GET SIX MINUTES TO YOURSELF: STUDY GUIDE

1. Is there a "perfect" woman in your life whom you are tempted to compare yourself to? Which of her qualities do you most admire?
2. Why are comparisons poisonous? Why, then, was this proverb included for us in the Scriptures?
3. Picture yourself trying to advise your child on the qualities of the perfect man or woman to marry. Which attributes would make the top of your list?
4. Read Proverbs 31 as a whole, in one sitting. What aspects of the woman do you most desire for yourself? Which ones do you already exemplify?
5. In motherhood, do you feel more like a valiant warrior or a battle-worn, wounded casualty? Why?
6. How can this ideal female standard be useful to your own journey in motherhood today?

---

* Ellen G. White, *The Adventist Home* (Hagerstown, MD: Review and Herald® Publishing Association, 2002), 232, 233; emphasis added.

Hands Full

Wow, do you ever have *your* hands full!" clucked the middle-aged lady in red high heels who stood behind me in the bank line. The twin on my hip cried loudly while I shushed even louder. The twin strapped onto my back repeatedly yanked my disheveled ponytail from side to side. Toby bent backwards to limbo under the retractable ropes as Caleb silently unhitched one from the post, knocking down the post, and Toby, resulting in screams and resounding clangs that made everyone stop and stare at me. Except for Madame Obvious in the heels. Staring didn't serve her well—no—she needed to stamp this moment with a witty comment.

Everywhere I go with my four kids, people say this exact same thing to me: "You sure have your hands full!" It happens all day long. I get this in line at the grocery store a *lot*—"Boy, Mama, don't you have your hands full! Heh heh!" People say this to me in the foyer at church as I'm herding the children into the sanctuary—a room far, far too quiet for my children. "Got your hands full, dontcha?" Strangers say this to me in parks and clothing stores and while passing me on the sidewalk. "Now there's a lady who has her hands full!" At a birthday party, when there were literally dozens of other kids crawling all over the house, a man singled me out and gestured to my four fighting together over the same toy in the corner, asking, "Are those all yours? You've got your hands full!" Even the teenage girl at the drive-through window had merely to glance into my bouncing car before she said, "Looks like you have your hands full there, oh my goodness." These people—all of them—they shift their eyebrows, they shake their heads, they laugh and they marvel. What am I, a freak show?

I mean, I get it—four kids is a lot; I'm kind of insane looking (and feeling) when I take them all out in public together. Having two-year-old twins is a lot, also—that's not something you see every day, apparently. And we are usually making a large enough scene to warrant this judgment call, to be sure. But I'm still surprised at how many times I hear it. On average, I am told I "have my hands full" usually by about three random people. Every. Single. Day.

It's not just in real life that people say this to me, either. The remark appears just as frequently on social media as well. A few weeks ago, I posted a story on Facebook relating the moment I simultaneously realized the house was silent of kid noises and heard the nearby sound of running water. I followed the telltale trickle into my master bathroom, where I found my twins, both fully clothed, splashing around a brimming bathtub in utter delight—and wearing bike helmets. I posted this story out of confusion, mostly. I expected people to laugh, or ask for pictures, or ponder what the bike helmets had anything to do with anything (as did I). But no. Instead, I received one statement over and over and over again. You guessed it: "My word, Melissa! YOU SURE HAVE YOUR HANDS FULL!!!"

But here's the icing on the cake: Last night as I crawled into bed, my foot hit something round, cold, and hard underneath the bed. It was late, and I was too tired to figure out what mysterious item lurked there, but I told myself I'd investigate in the morning. Daylight revealed that my foot had kicked a potato. But this rather large baking potato wasn't alone—oh no—there were ten others piled around it. Who shoved eleven potatoes under my bed? I asked my husband if he'd happened to see the culprit, and do you know what that man dared to say to me? He sighed. And then he admitted, "We really have our hands full, don't we?" ARE YOU KIDDING ME? *Et tu, Brutus?*

People make this observation as if it's clever, or original, as if they were the first person on the entire planet to ever think of it. As if nobody anywhere has ever told me, "You sure have your hands full!" Maybe they are trying to be funny, hoping that adding humor to a stressful situation will be appreciated (sometimes it is). Or perhaps they are so overwhelmed for me that they feel the need to reach out. It's possible they just feel amused. I've definitely seen admiration on peoples' faces, and sometimes even nostalgic stares. But I'm almost certain that they all go home thanking the good Lord above that they are not me, and maybe that's exactly why they say it in the first place—the sweet joy of comparison. Whatever the reason, I meet this wisecrack more times monthly than a mama wishes for a nap. So you can imagine how often that is.

What exactly is the proper response to this question? I never know what to say. What does one reply in answer to "You sure have your hands full"? I've tried sarcastic comebacks—"Oh, do I? Are those kids following me again?" Then I've sampled serious statements like, "Yes, I do. And it's really hard. I'm exhausted." Sometimes I'll retort, "Thanks for pointing that out," or fake a laugh, or look away in exasperation. I wish I possessed the courage to say things like, "Why don't you lend me a hand, then?" or "That's really not a helpful comment right now," or even "How do you think that makes me feel?" But none of these choices ever seem like the perfect acknowledgment. What are these people trying to tell me? And what should *I* say back?

Since I'm faced with this feedback daily (sometimes hourly), I've racked up a lot of time to think about a correct way to counter it. A while back, I started asking myself a different question: If I have my hands full, then exactly *what* do I have my hands full *of*? Believe it or not, the answers started coming in rapid-fire when I considered it that way. I kept my eyes open, kept my heart open. I let them fall on me and surround me and wrap me up in their lovely weight until I collected so many that I'd never have time to share them all in any single confrontation.

But I can write them. So here they are—here's what I'd say, if anyone ever gave me the time and attention to answer. This is how I would echo the ever-present "You've sure got your hands full!" exclamation, if I could:

Yes. I do have my hands full, don't I? But let me tell you what they are full of: My hands are full of extra coats and left shoes and diaper bag straps. My hands are full of emergency snacks and rainy-day backup plans. My hands hold miniature wrists and chubby bodies of people I actually *made*. Can I even *speak* what a *blessing* that is? My hands are full of cameras capturing memories I will treasure for a lifetime. My hands are full of new surprises every day. My hands are full of laughter and love—*so* much love, it's unmeasurable. My hands are full of cuddles and kisses and anytime snuggles. My hands are full of tears over tiny tragedies, and my hands are full of magic to heal any hurt. My hands are full of determination—the kind that crawls out of bed every half an hour, all night long, to hold the feverish throwing-up frame. My hands are full of scars, regrets of all the things I've done wrong and all the mistakes I've made. My hands are full of forgiveness—endless forgiveness—for each of my children forever, and almost for myself. My hands are full of their history—the first word, the first step, the first day of school, the first time he rode a bike, the first time she kissed my cheek. My hands are full of the rocks they bring me as prizes, full of pinecones and pretty leaves and sticks they just *knew* I'd love. My hands are full of crushed purple wildflowers she picked for me and skipped inside, piggy-tails bouncing, to deliver. My hands are full of broken toys and widowed socks and the prized stuffed animals they cannot sleep without. My hands are full of Tylenol and tooth-fairy money. My hands are full of cookie recipes and playdate times and Christmas present ideas. My hands are full of prayers. My hands are full of hopes for futures yet unwritten, dreams for safety and success, love and luck, happiness and heaven. My hands are full of fears for all I stand to lose, all the pain I cannot shield them from. My hands are full of humor, oh, so much humor! So many silly moments no one could ever count. My hands are full of wonder, watching brown eyes dance while life unfolds before them. My hands are full of faith in a man who loves me and faith in a God who never leaves me. My hands are full of the most precious gifts this world will ever give me. My hands are full of *life*, people! Life abundant, life complete, the blessings and the joy of the fullest life imaginable. My hands are full of the *privilege* of motherhood. And I love my full hands. I praise God for my full hands. I would not, not ever, have my hands *any* other way.

IN CASE YOU GET SIX MINUTES TO YOURSELF: STUDY GUIDE

1. Is there a particular comment that people repeatedly make about you?
2. Has anyone ever told you that you have your hands full? How did that make you feel? How did you respond?

3. As you consider how full your hands are, are you more likely to feel resentful, overwhelmed, discouraged, delighted, or grateful?

4. When you think of God as a parent to all of us, how does that change your picture of your own full hands?

5. What difficult things are your hands full of today? What beautiful things are your hands full of? Which of these things do you need to bring before God?

6. What, if anything, would you like to take out of your hands that you should no longer carry?

The Guilties

They were waiting for me at the doctor's office, but they're always waiting for me there, even though I try to do every single thing right: Have I been supplementing with vitamin D since we live in Seattle? Well, not really, no. Have I remembered to check the smoke detectors and childproof the cupboards containing medicines or chemicals, now that the twins are learning to walk? Well, yes, mostly, except the . . . oh, and that . . . ah. Nope. Haven't done those very well either. Well now, what about my son's nervous habits—licking his lips over and over until they turn dark red and crack, biting his nails till they bleed, clearing his throat incessantly. These habits are normal? Hallelujah! Wait, I shouldn't stress out about them so much—in fact, putting pressure on him to stop doing those things likely is making them worse? Oh. Oh my, oh no. It's certain. I knew it—I'm doing everything wrong! *They* were there at the doctor's, all right, boy were they ever there!

They ambushed me during the Christmas season too, when a girlfriend texted and said, "We are enjoying the holidays so much! Special treats and songs at night and lots of family memories! Is your family making time to treasure the holidays?" (Ladies, take note: this is not a nice text to send to a busy mommy.) I wanted terribly to respond with the truth: "No, in fact, we are not 'treasuring' anything. We are trying desperately just to make it! To get the kid to school on time, get food in all six of our tummies, keep enough dishes clean to eat on, scrape some money together to fund a trip across country and somehow still buy our children gifts, and then try to put up the tree and decorations in the midst of it all! But thank you, thanks so much for making me feel lousy about all the things we *should* be doing that we're *not* doing." And then—there *they* were. And right beside *them*, the lists. Lists of all the things we really ought to be doing—decorating gingerbread houses and cuddling by the fire and singing carols and enjoying hot chocolate while watching Christmas movies . . . sigh. *They* were heavy that day.

I was so disappointed when *they* managed to find me at church—the one place on earth I am supposed to be totally free of *them*! But *they* found me just the same. *They* appeared arm in arm with the music coordinator, who swooned, "Oh, I'm just *so* excited that we have a harpist in our church now! I told your husband I just *know* you'll be willing to play your harp for our Christmas concert, but he told me I had to ask you first—so will you?" Another pause. Another expectation I hadn't anticipated. "Uh, I have three broken strings," I replied sheepishly, "and besides—even if I order them and they do come in time, I haven't practiced in ten months. I don't even know when I would find the time to practice at all." Her face dropped, and *bam*—*they* are surrounding me in full force, suffocating me, sentencing me: *I am burying my talents in the ground. I am letting people down. I am not using my gifts to build up the church. I am a bad pastor's wife; so many other people could do this job so much better* . . . and on and on and on.

Even tonight, *they* were waiting for me at bedtime, lurking in the doorway of the twins' room when I tripped over the stack of books on the floor. Almost a full fifteen hours ago, my three-year-old son Toby had eagerly placed these books in my lap and asked whether I would read to him. I was nursing she-twin at the time, and he-twin was crying for his turn next, so I brushed Toby off in a fluster of "Later! Not now, sweetie! But I will definitely read them later." And I meant that too. But the smarting spot on my toe where the books just banged suddenly accused me of the truth: There was no later. Later never came. Now that it's too late and he's already in bed, I am able to remember—Toby standing beside me in his blue footsie pajamas, morning hair disheveled, precious blankie clutched in arm, just simply wanting some time and attention from his busy, distracted mommy. "You forgot him," *they* whisper, "for fifteen hours!" And *they* are right.

I hate *them*. *They* wait for me everywhere. Who are *they*? Oh come on—you know them well, don't you, Mama?

My good friend Angela calls *them* "the Guilties," and *they* show up whenever we find ourselves in a situation that seems to cause us guilt. *They* are the thoughts in our heads that tell us: You're guilty. "Guilty" is *their* constant mantra: guilty, guilty, guilty. *They* send us clear messages that say:

- Who I am is wrong.
- I'm not doing enough.
- I could and should be doing better.

This small insidious army of doubts bands together and systematically accuses us of crimes, attacks our peace of mind, holds hostage our self-worth, and strategically scatters our sense of joy. The Guilties are skilled at finding every single gap and hole in our mommy armor. *They* always seem to know right where we're weak, and *they* find a myriad ways in which we can fail. Haven't you heard *them* chanting at you as well? Haven't you felt *their* advance? I suppose *they* follow some of us more faithfully than others . . .

This isn't just a problem with women, by the way. After Angela introduced me to the Guilties (though I already knew them), I started asking other people whether they knew the Guilties as well. Most of the mothers I asked were well acquainted. But what was surprising to me was that most of the fathers I asked were also in touch with the Guilties. Here are some of the things those daddies admitted to me:

- "I wish I could be a better provider for my family. I wish I made a larger income, had a more successful career, a bigger home and nicer things."
- "I feel guilty when I don't make enough time in my day to connect with my wife."
- "I feel sad that I just can't spend more time with my kids. I feel like I'm cheating them."
- "I really hate myself when I admit that I just don't like my kids sometimes."
- "Compared to other dads, I'm really not as athletic, engaging, or fun."
- "There is no guilt as bad as when I make my wife cry."
- "I feel guilty when I want to pursue my own dreams and interests at the cost of my family."
- "I condemn myself when I spend three hours playing video games on a Sunday instead of doing work around the house."
- "It's disappointing when I realize that I'm not keeping up with my friends from college."
- "I feel guilty that I don't do enough for the church."
- "I feel guilty when I realize that I am not living up to my full potential."

Guilty, guilty, guilty, guilty—*they* chant louder than any mob.

But the Guilties don't even stop with our marriage and family life—oh no. They are quite famous for coming between relationships with other mothers and women too. Instead of celebrating the obvious talents and attributes of a friend, we choose instead to let the Guilties remind us that *we* are not very good at those things. If a woman makes a delicious food dish for a party, for example—rather than compliment her, we bemoan our own plain food and lack of cooking skills. A friend decorates her house beautifully for a holiday, but instead of gushing over her skill, we feel "lesser" because our house is not decorated so well. When a slender, beautiful, well-dressed woman walks into a room, our envy doesn't permit us to admire her or encourage her for the hard work it took to look so nice, because we feel too guilty about how our own appearance pales in comparison. The Guilties, you see, have stolen from us the ability to truly love, accept, and celebrate the women around us.

Because I am a Christian, I know that the Guilties are not just my voice alone.

There's another name for that voice in my head speaking lies. Another explanation exists for the ridiculous amounts of guilt that I sometimes carry around with me. The true source of the Guilties just so happens to be a very, very old voice . . .

> Then war broke out in heaven. Michael and his angels fought against the dragon, and the dragon and his angels fought back. But he was not strong enough, and they lost their place in heaven. The great dragon was hurled down—that ancient serpent called the devil, or Satan, who leads the whole world astray. He was hurled to the earth, and his angels with him.
> Then I heard a loud voice in heaven say:
> "Now have come the salvation and the power
>   and the kingdom of our God,
>   and the authority of his Messiah.
> For the accuser of our brothers and sisters,
>   who accuses them before our God day and night,
>   has been hurled down" (Revelation 12:7–10).

Before any of us were born, Satan was accusing. Before the first woman became the first imperfect mother, Satan was accusing. Even before God created the earth, Satan was accusing God Himself—of being unfair. He has been accusing since the beginning of time as we know it, and he will be accusing until the end of time on this earth. He never stops, never ceases, never gives up, accusing us "day and night," as the text says. This phrase portrays a constant action, a consistency of accusing whenever the opportunity presents itself—I can just *feel* this, can't you? "To accuse" is a legal term; it means the act of listing sins, bringing up grievances, collecting a case full of all the things done wrong. This sounds *exactly* like the Guilties! And it is. Satan, the "accuser," is the original voice behind the Guilties.

But the trouble with pinning all guilt onto Satan is that guilt is actually a good thing gone wrong. We buy into it so easily because we know that our guilt is really based on good, wholesome desires: I want to read to my son, I want to steal some moments to snuggle him on my lap and bury my nose in his hair's Toby-scent. I want to keep my kids healthy and safe, I want to create special holiday memories, and I really do want to use my talents and my gifts for Jesus. We all want to be good parents, good providers, and beneficial individuals to society. These desires to give the best of our energies are good things! Good, that is, until the Guilties get ahold of them. Then, these tools for positive change get twisted into crippling evidences against us, proof that we are not enough.

Guilt in motherhood can often be overblown, I admit, but sometimes it is also legitimately telling us that something needs to change. True guilt is a function of intimacy—it works to push us back *into* a relationship when the relationship has been threatened. If I really have been neglecting my child's needs, guilt is in place to help me realize that and make adjustments. I wouldn't want to ignore this kind of guilt; I want to respond to it. In the same way, guilt is our tether to God, a pain mechanism that lets us know we've sinned and we need to repent. God uses the conviction of sin freely—think of His exchanges with the Pharisees, or with the woman caught in adultery. He doesn't hesitate to call sin by its rightful name, but He doesn't stop there. "Go, and sin no more," is where God's guilt leads, meaning, let this recognition of your sins inspire you to make changes. It is supposed to drive us back *to* Him, not away from Him.

But this doesn't always happen, does it? True conviction transforms into the treacherous Guilties when Satan hijacks the guilt. And when Satan gets ahold of guilt, he turns it into something else, something very different, something we know as *shame*. Shame goes far beyond guilt—shame is the tearing down of our sense of self. Shame doesn't just tell us we've done wrong, shame tells us that we are hopeless, worthless, unlovable, and beyond the ability to change our ways. Shame is condemnation without the hope of repair. And shame is the true voice of the accuser. God never shames us. We will never find God attacking our self-worth. On the contrary, we find God on the cross, showing us just exactly how much we *are* worth.

I want to make sure that I can tell the difference between the guilt of conviction and the shame of the Guilties. How do I discern when I really need to make changes from when I just need to stop accepting lies? A good method of discernment is to check the driving direction: guilt drives us *to* God, or it's not *from* God. So if it's driving us away from God, Satan is certainly the driver. Satan's constant goal is to destroy our connection with Jesus and to destroy our identity and worth in the process. If my guilt is telling me to improve and run to Jesus, I can listen. But if my guilt is telling me I'm worthless and He'll never accept me—that, ladies, is the voice of the accuser.

I wish this chapter on the Guilties could end here, but it can't. We aren't finished yet. Because even after all that's been said, there's still another voice out there, and this voice is perhaps the deadliest of all.

"Who's accusing you?" the seminary professor questioned our class suddenly. We were elbows deep in the study of the book of Revelation, looking at Satan, the ultimate accuser of the brethren (and sisteren), when Dr. Paulien suddenly asked this. People began answering immediately.

"Satan!"

"The devil!"

"That serpent of old!"

"No," Dr. Paulien answered patiently. "Who's accusing you?"

The pastors got creative. If it wasn't Satan, the obvious answer, then who was it?

"My teachers!" one responded.

"The government!" exclaimed another.

"The DMV," admitted a man in the back.

"My wife! Constantly!" someone blurted out, and the whole class laughed. My husband poked me jokingly from the seat to my left and raised his eyebrows at me. I grinned at him as Dr. Paulien answered, "Well, good point with the wife—we'll pray for you, pastor! But no, seriously—who's accusing you?"

"Family."

"Neighbors."

"Friends."

"Enemies." The answers kept coming in rapid-fire.

"My loan companies."

"Church members!"

"The conference office."

"My head pastor."

"My assistant pastor."

"My youth pastor."

"My secretary."

As the possibilities slowly got checked off one by one, I began sitting lower in my chair, and ever so slightly ducking my head, wanting to go unnoticed. Because I knew the answer, or, I thought I did. But it was an answer I didn't want to give. Especially not in front of a whole room full of pastors.

Systematically, Dr. Paulien worked his way through the entire class of pastors, asking each one, "Who's accusing you?" Nobody seemed to have the answer he was looking for, though everyone did have an answer. It wasn't the church, it wasn't our in-laws, and it wasn't even the media. Instinctively, I began to feel that he was saving me for last.

I was right.

I remember seeing the shadow of his tall form crossing over my desk and my bowed head. He paused, before stating, "For some reason, it is usually only the women in my class who answer this question correctly." Another pause. I raised my head and there he was, waiting for my gaze to meet his, looking me directly in the eye. "Melissa," he began slowly, "please tell us. Who's accusing you today?"

I took a breath. My heart knew the truth. "Me," I answered softly. "I am accusing me."

"Bingo," he replied.

The class fell silent in a knowing sort of way—a silence that speaks conviction. We all knew. We were all living under the harshest accusers of them all: ourselves. He went on to explain that day that we have taken over Satan's job for him. *We* become the accusers! Oh, it's so true, isn't it? Didn't we know this from the beginning? We do such a wonderful job of accusing and condemning ourselves that often the devil likely has no need to add to it. He can suggest one fatal lie, and we will take it from there—get out the whipping post and continuously beat ourselves. Wallow and drown in pools of self-hatred, guilt, and shame. We are the ones who let the Guilties follow us all day and all night long.

If this is true—and I know it is—then here's my question: How can we possibly *ever* break free? If we are living not only under the attacks of the accuser, but the accuser is also our own internal voices of shame, then how do we ever stand a chance to liberate ourselves from the Guilties?

I actually didn't finish the text about the dragon in Revelation earlier (I know, how rude—I'm guilty!), but now I will. Here's the rest of it, and here's the end of the matter:

> "They triumphed over him [the dragon]
>> by the blood of the Lamb,
>> and by the word of their testimony" (Revelation 12:11a).

What does this even mean? How can blood and a testimony overcome so much that haunts us, so much every day that we can't ever seem to break free of? The blood of the lamb is living proof that Jesus Christ has died for us. He has forgiven us from all the guilty things we have done and ever will do—real or imagined. So when Satan (the voice of shame) tries to tear down our worth and our identity as women and mothers, we can cling to the cross as our true identity. We can insist that we are *not* worthless, we are daughters of the King, worth the priceless gift of Jesus' blood. It's not our looks or our talents or our cooking and decorating skills or even our parenting skills that bring us our worth. No, mommies, our worth is found in Jesus alone. If we anchor our worth in Him, nothing and no one else can ever take it away from us.

The second way to overcome the accuser and the Guilties is by "the word of our testimony"—our story of what God has done for us and all that He *continues* to do for us each day. He changes my selfish heart and slowly shapes my rough character, He invites me into His presence, He speaks to my soul, He gives me guidance and wisdom, and He fills me with a peace and a joy that I didn't ever know before Him. This is powerful! We can overcome the accuser, the king of the Guilties, with the story of all that God has done for us. We need to get good at telling these stories. When Satan tries to accuse us of what we're doing wrong, we've got to get good at reminding him of what God is doing right.

So who's accusing you today, Mother? Are you haunted by the Guilties? Is the accuser speaking lies of shame over you? Or have you taken over the accuser's job for him, speaking accusations against your own identity? Take time to remember that your value lies in the cross of Jesus. Find moments to reflect on the word of your testimony—your very own story of what Jesus has done for you. We were never meant to live under the reign of the the Guilties. We were meant to be free.

IN CASE YOU GET SIX MINUTES TO YOURSELF: STUDY GUIDE

1. In what situations do the Guilties most often show up for you? Are these things you should really feel guilty about?

2. Can you relate to the author's story in her seminary class—are you accusing yourself?

3. Can you tell the difference in your life between God's conviction and Satan's shame?

4. What does it mean to find your worth in the blood of Jesus? Is this really going to protect you from comparing yourself to other women and feeling worthless? Why?

5. What is the "word of your testimony"? What is your unique story of what Jesus has done for you?

6. What are the lies the accuser has been speaking over you?

7. Is there anything God might be asking you to change today?

Waves

July

"Come play with me, Mommy!" Caleb exclaims. "Come jump in the waves, it's *so-o-o-o-o-o* fun!" His bony body glistens with salt water and sand, and his smile is practically jumping off his face. A summer day at the beach—childhood at its best. The invitation is too contagious; I must accept, yes, even though it means parading down the beach in this bikini I had no business wearing.

"OK, buddy, Mommy would love to jump waves with you! Let's go!"

We race down Daytona Beach to the water's edge and leap into the ocean, laughing and giggling already. "Come out farther, Mommy! Out to the *re-e-e-e-ally* big waves!" Caleb insists, and I follow. Warm water waves crash over our chests and shoulders, and we inch farther out.

When he can barely tippy-toes-touch the bottom, we stop moving forward and face the waves defiantly. They surge and crest and tumble over us again and again. I am soaking wet, and I am laughing out loud. Time bends, and I feel like a child again. Was it really so long ago? We plunge wildly under the surf, we hurtle ourselves headlong into the heart of the waves, holding our breaths, over and over again.

"Hold my hand, Mommy!" Caleb shrieks in delight, and I do—instantly I do. At seven years old, he doesn't often anymore ask to hold my hand, so I hold it like a prize.

"*Re-a-a-a-a-ady* . . . jump!" he sings, and we spring up together, hand in hand, mommy and son, through the surge. "*Who-o-o-o-o-h-o-o-o-o-o-o-o-o-o!*" I whoop and holler. "We made it—oh!—here comes another one, ready? *Ju-u-u-u-ump!*"

"I love this day, Mommy! This is the best day of the whole summer!" he cheers, pushing our hands into the air as another wave approaches. And I think, *Yes, yes it is.*

My cousin left today for her honeymoon in Paris. Two of my friends are taking a cruise in the Caribbean, and another is at a resort in Jamaica. But as for me, there's nowhere else I'd rather be in all the world than here on the beach with my boy, jumping the waves.

August

Toby and I sit together at a small, cast-iron table on the patio of the painting studio. This is our date, just him and me. He's chosen to paint a small ceramic owl, and I selected a spoon holder for the kitchen. He's painting the owl's head splotches of red, green, and gold, while I obsess over which green to use for my palm tree. He is chattering endlessly, happy and excited.

"This is super fun, Mommy! I just love painting! Did you know I'd love painting? I'm pretty good at painting. Look at my owl, Mommy!"

The owl winks at me with black and red eyes, and I love it already. When I see it sitting on a shelf, I know I'll think back on this day with thankfulness.

"Maybe when I am a pickle farmer, I will also build a painting store on my farm," Toby speculates, planning his future. I laugh.

"What a good idea, sweetie! Can Mommy come visit your farm and pick pickles?"

"Every day, Mommy!" he orders. "And we can paint owls too!"

Is the smile jumping off my face? It sure feels like it. Waves of contentment crash over me.

I look across the small patio and see a woman in the coffee shop beside us, feet propped up on a chair, face tilted slightly to the sun, mind lost in a good book. Normally, on every other day of the year, I would envy this woman terribly. But not today.

Today, I am painting pottery with my sweet boy and planning a pickle farm, and there's nowhere else I'd rather be in all the world.

September

Giggling twins in full footsie pajamas fall on me from both sides, hugging me and rolling over me. It's past their bedtime, but I'm still sitting here on the floor with them because I can't get enough of their laughter tonight.

Wyatt sets up four water bottles strategically, glances up at me to make sure I'm watching, and then squeals for joy as he kicks each one over. "Naughty feet!" he chuckles. "Naughty feet!"

"Oh, naughty feet!" I agree and tickle the little feet, legs, and tummy. Such silly games they make up, but I love them.

Brooke places a plastic string of hot pink pearls over her head and croons, "*Pe-e-eety*, Mommy!"

"So *pe-e-eety*!" I assure her, and she is, she's the most beautiful person on earth.

"Mommy!" she exclaims as she collapses into my lap, burying her tiny head in my arms, "*Wuv* you." Waves of love leap up in me, and my heart is so full it could burst.

It's deadline week, and I know I should be writing—my manuscript will likely suffer because of it. But I can't help it. My arms are full of squirming, happy twins, and there's truly nowhere else I'd rather be in all the world.

"Better is one day in your courts than a thousand elsewhere," claims the singer to the Lord in Psalm 84:10, and I know what he's thinking. I understand. I know that sometimes you can be in Someone's presence and know for certain that there's nowhere, not anywhere else in all the world, you'd rather be.

IN CASE YOU GET SIX MINUTES TO YOURSELF: STUDY GUIDE

1. What were some of your favorite experiences with your children, when you thought to yourself, *There's nowhere else in all the world I'd rather be?*
2. Have you ever felt this way in God's presence? When? What was happening?
3. Read Psalm 84. What is the meaning of verse 10 in the context of the whole chapter?
4. How deeply does your own soul crave an experience with Jesus today?

Foodies

She walked into my room barefoot, in her pink gingham dress and rosebud barrettes, gingerly holding a large, empty ceramic bowl in her tiny hands. She carefully, silently placed the bowl in my lap, on top of the keyboard where my hands rested. She looked up at me then, expectantly, and blinked her beautiful brown eyes several times. What was this supposed to mean—this empty blue bowl? Finally, seeing that I needed a much clearer explanation, she pointed twice at the bowl and whispered with a smile, "Foodies, Mommy!"

Oh! Food! My precious girl felt hungry. I glanced at my clock. How did it get so far past lunchtime already? How long had I been writing? When was the last time any of us had eaten, and what food was there in the house to even make?

"Foodies," she repeated again decisively, reminding me that the bowl was still empty. "Foodies, Mommy. Now."

This is me today, God, bringing my empty bowl before You and saying, "Food! Feed me please!" I'm heart-hungry, Father, and my bowl has been so empty for so long. It doesn't have to be a banquet—I'd gladly take a snack or even a side dish. But please, please fill me today.

What am I hungry for? Oh—I do have a menu, actually, but You made it. Here it is:

I'm hungry for *love.* All kinds of love, Father, love in many flavors. I want to shower my children with love, and my husband. I need Your love pouring into me when I'm ready to respond with other things, like anger or frustration. What else— oh—I'd like to love myself more. I wish I had enough love to spread around to all the hurting people I run into every day. Most of all, though, I need to bask in the warmth of Your love. To let it fill me and feed me.

Another thing I'm hungry for is *joy.* Not just happiness—that's as fleeting as a mood—but real joy, Father. The kind of joy that comes only from You. The kind of joy that nothing else can take away. Joy just in the everyday, menial tasks that I must perform. I know it's my job to be the joy-infuser in this home, to fill it up with joy overflowing, but I can't do that unless You fill me first. So, please, I'd like joy.

Peace would be an amazing treat as well. I don't mean the absence of chaos or bickering; I know it's unrealistic to expect that. But the peace like the calm in the midst of a storm, that peace that passes understanding that You talk about—I want that. I'd like peace about my future, and peace about my children's futures as well.

If You aren't really offering an all-you-can-eat buffet today, Lord, and I only get to pick one thing, I'd like to ask for *patience* most of all. Because this is what I lack, most of all—oh, how I crave it. It's so easy to lose my patience, and I do it far too often. But my impatience hurts these precious little hearts I've been entrusted with, and I feel so awful when I hurt them. Please give me patience for every minute of every day, because that's how often I need it. It's not something I can cultivate in myself, because I've tried, Lord. It's Yours to give, so give it to me, I beg.

Kindness is something I could use a little bit more of as well. Sometimes I am matter-of-fact but not kind. Sometimes I am short and snippy and anything but kind. This is so sad, because my words mean so much to these little people. I want to always treat my family with kindness, and anyone else I come in contact with, too, for that matter. I know that kindness is one of the marks of a Christian, so when I'm rude, I think I don't speak very well for You, God. Give me kindness, and the eyes to know when to use it.

Since I know I need to stop chasing after perfection, I'd be satisfied simply with *goodness.* And I'm not really sure what You originally meant by goodness, but I know what kind of goodness I need: I need to be a good mommy, good wife, good friend, good Christian, good daughter, good sister, and good person. I want to have a good heart. I desire for my motives to be good, and even for my thoughts to be good. (I know, this is asking a lot—am I getting greedy? I told You I was *very* hungry . . .)

Something I really, really hunger for is *faithfulness.* I notice how often my heart strays from You, God, and I'm ashamed. I want to be faithful to all You have called me to, all the responsibilities You have placed in my lap. Some days I'm faithful only to my own agenda and selfishness. But I want to faithfully train my children to serve You, Lord. Help me to be as faithful in my encouragement of them as I am in my corrections. I want to be faithful to my husband in every word and thought. I want to be faithful to the plans You have prepared for me and faithfully seek to discover them more every day.

I'm hungry for *gentleness* as well. Gentleness in touch, speech, and action. Teach my hands to gently soothe the child throwing a temper tantrum, when it would be much more cathartic to use harshness. Show me how to be gentle with my children's feelings, and with their developing personalities. Instruct me on how to gently guide them to You in ways that won't feel like brainwashing, force, or manipulation. Give me gentleness in all my encounters.

The last thing on my menu today, Lord, is *self-control.* You'd think that after all these years I wouldn't still be chasing self-control, but I am. And granted, I don't struggle with it in the same ways I did as a child or a teen, but yet here I am still yearning for it. Give me self-control over my bad habits and distracted tendencies. Grant me self-control to hold my tongue when other mommies express their obviously wrong opinions. Send self-control to me in those split seconds after I've been hurt, offended, or challenged, right before I'm making the decision on how to react. And give me enough self-control to fight for the space in my busy schedule to seek You daily, my Father.

Love, joy, peace, patience, kindness, goodness, faithfulness, gentleness, and self-control—the fruits of Your Spirit, Lord. I've wasted a lot of time trying to grow these things in myself, and time and time again I fail. And that's because these aren't things I can accomplish simply by working harder to get them. These are gifts from You. Fruits, to be exact—things that You cultivate in us and bring to life through us. They are the result of the presence of Your Spirit, and so they cannot be grown without that presence. I don't know how they grow, but I know that I have to spend time in Your presence to make it possible.

It's no surprise that the best things about all of us don't originate from inside of us. All the character traits I'm the most proud of—my ability to love, my contagious sense of joy, my friendly kindness—I thought these were traits of my own character, but when I realize how easily they can disappear, I know they're not. They are blessings that only You can bestow, Father. So fill me with these foods, as full as You can, as completely as I will let You.

IN CASE YOU GET SIX MINUTES TO YOURSELF: STUDY GUIDE

1. Do you ever forget to feed your children, pets, or yourself? What happens when you do?
2. Spiritually speaking, do you feel full, satisfied, hungry, or starving today?
3. Which fruits of the Spirit do you crave the most? Where are you the most lacking?
4. Is it true that God supplies the best character traits in all of us? If so, what does this mean for your quest to become a better person?
5. How does the presence of the Spirit grow these fruits in us?
6. What gifts from God are you most hungering for today?

Seasons

Spring

Two heartbeats on the ultrasound!!! I can't believe it—we are having twins! Oh, I'm just in awe, I'm amazed, I don't know what to say! Two babies at once!

I did see the first heartbeat flickering on the screen, but then there was something funny right beside it blinking too—my kidneys or something? Who can make sense of those blurry ultrasounds? "Greg, you better come take a look at this," he urged my husband from out of his chair. "What is that other thing there?" I asked Dr. Edstrom insistently, and he chuckled when he said, "It's another baby!" I just laughed and laughed and laughed. What else can you do at a time like that?

I always wanted to have twins. I thought it sounded so festive and fun. But now I can't believe it's really happening to me! Two little babies at the same time. This will double the amount of children we presently have. What a glorious blessing—two new little people. New life is all around me today, it feels like I'm waking up to a brand-new beginning, and the future looks incredible!

Winter

I drove away from the hospital tonight without my brand-new baby twins. Left them in plastic boxes, alone, with tubes in them, fighting to live, because there wasn't a room for me. Left them! I had to leave my babies. My heart could hardly bear it. I was trembling in sorrow as Greg led me away.

But then I came home to my precious Summer—bleeding and dying on the living room floor. My first "child." She has been my constant companion through more than any human could ever know, the best dog a girl could ever have. I couldn't even bend down to hug her, my C-section stitches hurt so bad from being literally ripped apart for the emergency early birth. We took her to the vet, and she died in my arms, with her head on my shoulder.

I have no tears left, I've cried them all. And Caleb—how he shook with despair as he cried for her. He prayed for that dog every single night for five months. I am crushed, I am hollow. Hold me, Jesus, because I'm shaking, shaking like a leaf. My heart will never, never heal.

Summer

Today we stood on the mountaintops—and I do mean that literally! Our whole family hiked Excelsior Pass in Mount Baker National Forest, all six miles, to the top and back! I was so proud of the boys—Toby leading the way with his Batman backpack bouncing behind him, Caleb skipping stones for the twins in the river, holding a baby's hand or wildly running to the first patch of snow we saw. Brooke and Wyatt rode happily in their packs for the most part, but when we let them walk, they followed the older boys eagerly down the trail. We passed reflection lakes, clear as glass, surrounded by rugged old boardwalks. We wound through deep forests that opened out into glorious green meadows full of wildflowers, butterflies, and bees. The boys ran with me through the tall grass as we sang, "The hills are alive . . . !" *

We summited the pass just before sunset, where we ate our picnic lunches, took wild photos, and watched the mountain ranges in every direction turn to brilliant pinks, oranges, and golds. We could see all the way into Canada! The summer wind whipped through our hair as we sat shoulder to shoulder, and I felt so alive, so fully alive! We hiked down through the twilight, using our headlamps at the very end, and Toby held my hand the whole way so that I "wouldn't fall."

Once back at the parking lot, I spread out the old picnic blanket on the dirt ledge and we lay down together, all six of us, to watch for shooting stars. I pointed out the summer sky constellations—the big dipper, Cygnus, Cassiopeia, and Pegasus. Caleb found Vega and the North Star on his own. Wyatt kept exclaiming, "Star! Star!" as his chubby toddler fingers pointed above. And as we finally loaded the sleepy, happy children into the car for the drive home, I scooped up Brooke into my arms for a spontaneous midsummer night's dance. Suddenly then, my heart just welled up with joy and I whispered into her tiny ear, "Sometimes, little girl, life is this *good!" And I meant it—heart and soul.*

Fall

The winds of change are blowing in today, and I can feel our lives ebbing and altering once again. Greg received a call from an old friend today, with an invitation to come and minister alongside him as the pastoral care associate at his large church. Greg's eyes instantly lit up with passion and purpose at the thought, and just like that, everything that seemed so rock-solid and stable in our lives began shifting.

If we took it, we would begin the new year in a giant metropolitan east-coast city, not

---

* Oscar Hammerstein II, "The Sound of Music," from *The Sound of Music* (1959 Broadway musical).

here in the trees of this Pacific Northwest forest. Caleb would start a new school, we would leave our beautiful home, and we would say goodbye to all of our friends. These are heavy things, hard things, and yet, excitement is bubbling under the surface as well—new friends, a new town, new adventures, and a fresh new ministry position—maybe even for both of us! I have waited so long for that. But I've finally become content here at home too.

It's so hard to know when to let the old die out and when to embrace the new. It's difficult to get caught between two places. I fear things will get colder for us, for a while, as we try to explore this new option. But we've lived so many good days here already, and we've started itching for a change. It just might be time for a new season.

Of all the times in life that a woman must navigate through, motherhood is one of the most changing. There are seasons of such highs, and valleys of such lows. There are times of uncertainty mixed with intervals of peace, darks of depression that give way to such joy. And the way they come in such quick succession, one trailing right behind on the heels of another, can be both exhilarating and exhausting. One minute we feel amazing, the next we feel awful—and finally, we feel confused and crazy. Through all of this, we bear the constant pressure to produce—to keep doing more, being more, creating more, and contributing more to everyone and everything around us.

Into the nonstop expectations of this ever-changing landscape of our lives, what words of comfort and direction does our God speak? Consider the verses that begin my all-time favorite book of the Bible, and certainly the book containing the widest range of feeling changes in all of Scripture: the Psalms.

> Blessed is the woman
> who does not walk in step with the wicked
> or stand in the way that sinners take
> or sit in the company of mockers,
> but whose delight is in the law of the LORD,
> and who meditates his law day and night.
> She is like a tree planted by streams of water,
> which yields its fruit in season
> and whose leaf does not wither—
> whatever she [does] prospers (Psalm 1:1–3; gender pronouns
> altered).

At first this text doesn't seem relevant at all. But once, I found myself studying it during a particularly dark and empty time in my past, and a single thought stuck out to me so sharply: the thought that there are seasons.

Yes, there are seasons for rooting deep and growing tall and bearing lots of beautiful, showy fruit—of course. But some seasons? Some seasons are winter. Some seasons are just for hunkering down, healing, and huddling tight while the Son finds a way to melt that blanket of ice off the heart's branches. The freedom this gave me was huge, because I realized that I don't have to be constantly producing fruit. Sometimes it's OK just to rest and recover. Sometimes it's acceptable to be buried in ice. And sometimes, even small budding leaves can be an enormous sign of growth. Even the varied motions of the verbs in the text—walk, stand, sit—hint of seasons and changes and different states of being.

What is the secret to surviving the seasons? The text makes some suggestions: walk in God's ways, delight in His laws, meditate constantly on His teachings. These things root us deep. These practices anchor us to underground streams of living waters that continue to nourish and strengthen us, in spite of whatever weather may be brewing outside.

What season do you find yourself in today, mother? Are you on summertime's mountaintop? Riding the changing winds of autumn? Do you feel the pressures to constantly continue bearing fruit, even as your own limbs are drying and lifeless inside? Take heart, tired lady. Some seasons are winter. Some seasons are simply for God to grow *you*. Root yourself deep, sister—into the never-ending streams of God's amazing grace. The seasons may change around us, but our God never does. Summer, spring, winter, fall—God is faithful through them all.

IN CASE YOU GET SIX MINUTES TO YOURSELF: STUDY GUIDE

1. Which season has always been your favorite? Why? Which one do you dislike the most?
2. What are some spiritual seasons that your life has recently experienced?
3. Do you agree that some seasons are winter, that sometimes it's OK not to be contributing and producing? If not, why not?
4. Read the entire chapter of Psalm 1. How are the righteous contrasted with the wicked, and why is this comparison important?
5. Which season is your soul living in today? How do you need the Master Gardener to care for you in this season?

Sand

It's not very often a moment so magical appears unplanned out of creeping despair. Slowly descending the steps from the windy bluff down to the beach, my husband and I spoke in hushed tones to each other.

"Remember our walk two years ago down this same beach at midnight?" I asked.

"How could I forget?" Greg replied. "We sprawled on the sand and talked about how miserable we both were."

Neither of us said anything for a moment as we wound through the maze of driftwood logs, recalling one of the hardest years in all our lives.

"Things are better now," I ventured, "don't you think?"

"Oh, of course!" he exclaimed. "*So* much better! But still . . . it's not exactly . . ." he trailed off.

"I agree," I finished knowingly, "I'm still not completely happy either."

"What's wrong?" he asked, "Is it us? Are we still damaged from the hurt we shouldered before? Are we jaded? Or are we those awful kinds of people who are just never happy, no matter where they go?"

I pondered his questions for a moment as we shuffled heavily through thick sand, heading toward the surf breaking in the distance. Not even a beach vacation can fill the places in us that long for a deeper satisfaction, I realized.

"I think God is healing us," I suggested tentatively, "but I still don't think we are living life the way we truly want to. I think we are still unhappy. Missing something."

"Yeah," he agreed. "Something is still off. We're healing, but not quite there yet."

Saying it out loud made it seem so much more real. Why weren't we completely happy? After all these years in ministry, why were we still struggling every day? Why hadn't we found our places—those sweet spots that make one come alive and blossom with purpose? Over the years, we have watched more and more colleagues find their perfect fits in ministry. Or did they really? Maybe those perfect fits don't really exist, I speculated. Maybe everyone still struggles significantly, because true ministry is not about our own happiness but about servanthood and sacrifice and spending all your energy to see souls saved. It seems heroic, selfless, scary, and grim, all at the same time.

I wrestled with these thoughts as we left the dry sand and hit the wet, feet slapping against firmly packed sediment and shells. I thought of God's promise to do "a new thing" for us after the old has passed:

> "Forget the former things;
>   do not dwell on the past.
> See, I am doing a new thing!
>   Now it springs up; do you not perceive it?
> I am making a way in the wilderness
>   and streams in the wasteland" (Isaiah 43:18, 19).

He said this when Israel was in captivity. Sometimes, I feel my soul in captivity too. I don't want to dwell on the past. I've lived too long in the desert, wandered weary in this wasteland.

"I want something new, God," I silently prayed, "like You promised them. Do something new for us, pluck us from the past and do a new thing." I wondered if and when we could expect Him to do this "new thing" for us.

All of a sudden Greg grabbed my wrist forcefully and exclaimed, "Look down! Look down! Look down!"

I froze. Fear caught in my throat, and immediately my eyes dropped. Below me the sand sparkled in silvery-neon pinpoints for just a second, and then they disappeared. Did I imagine it? I took a step, and hundreds of tiny glowing sparkles shot out from my feet in every direction. Then vanished again. Another step—same thing.

"Bioluminescence!" he exclaimed, only to be met with my scientifically challenged blank stare. "The plankton, you know? They release light energy when they react with oxygen. Just look at them here, oh, and here!" And finally I understood. The thin layer of water upon the sand contained millions of tiny organisms that reacted when disturbed by my footsteps. Which meant that more footsteps would equal more light . . .

Awe overtook us. We forgot our status as adults—we whooped and hollered and laughed out loud. We jumped and ran and danced, every step sending sprays of luminescent light. I've never seen anything like it, not on all the beaches in all the countries I've ever traveled to.

After only a few moments of this wonder, I thought of them—my boys curled in sleeping bags, drifting to sleep in the cabin on the bluff. "We have to get them!" And he knew who I meant; we were running back before anyone could explain any more. Nothing makes a moment more full of magic for me than sharing it with my children. Breathless, we burst in and roused Caleb and Toby from recent sleepiness. "Come see! Come see!" we sang. "The beach is glowing! You won't believe it!" They were whiny at first, complaining and cold, but they followed us out into the night. I could sense the adventure growing for them as we descended the stairs to the shore and ran out wildly, chasing the tide to the water's edge.

The sand didn't glow at all, at first. And then farther on there were only a few glittery sparkles. But suddenly they burst into flickering lights in dazzling displays, and we found ourselves hopping and spinning free. The boys were entranced. "Mommy! Look! Glowing sand! Mommy, it sparkles! Watch me jump, Mommy! Run with me!" So we ran together, hand in hand, the plankton exploding ahead of us like fireworks in a festive night sky. We twirled and jogged in place, chased glowing circles of glimmering brilliance. It was one of the most magical experiences of my life.

"I love this, Mommy!" Caleb shrieked for joy as he shook my hands in celebration. And I knew then that the moment would follow me forever, to every beach I walked on in every night in any season.

I don't know how long we stayed, but we couldn't tear ourselves away. We pretended we were Elsa and the sand was turning to ice crystals beneath our feet. We talked about walking the streets of gold in heaven someday. "I feel so important!" someone said, laughing, because every step mattered, every foot sent sprays of light across the surface. I ran as fast as I could, trying to place my feet far in front of me so I was running on a path of glitter, a road of diamonds. Just as quickly as they lit up, though, they disappeared, in seconds. So we had to keep stomping, running, jumping, and dancing. The Olympic peninsula stretched out in miles of sandy beach ahead and behind, a late August moon setting in a haze over the Pacific. We transformed into Disney princesses, warriors with superpowers and magic feet, ninjas of the sand, Jedi Knights zooming through twinkling starry skies. In my own mind I became a traveler in a far-off forest, where fairy flower girls threw handfuls of glitter at my feet and led me down imaginary wedding aisles in the midnight moonlight. The enchanted midsummer night seemed almost from a dream, yet it was real and we were there.

My boys' squeals and giggles blended with the crashing waves glowing their own radiant shades of neon blue and green, and my heart swelled right along with the surf—full of love for them, full of gratefulness for this magic, for this moment, for this gift. I couldn't have planned it. But nobody had to show us how to enjoy it. We were not parents and children then. For just that sacred time, we were kids together, wild and free, "one with the wind and sky."*

It didn't hit me until we were back in the darkened cabin, brushing sand off tiny feet and planting kisses on sweaty foreheads. "Thank You, Jesus, for that very special

---

* Kristen Anderson-Lopez and Robert Lopez, "Let It Go," performed by Idina Menzel in *Frozen* (Burbank, CA: Walt Disney Disney Studios, 2014), DVD.

present!" I whispered in Toby's ear, and it returned, the verse: "See, I am doing a new thing! Now it springs up; do you not perceive it?" Instantly, the whole experience was more than just a happy memory for me. It felt like more like a promise. It felt like God was whispering, *"See, Melissa? I can make 'magic' out of nowhere. I can bring you joy you could never imagine. I can do a 'new thing' for you when the time is right. Trust Me. Wait on Me."*

The verse doesn't say He will take us out of the deserts or wastelands—it says He will do a new thing *within* them: "I am making a way in the wilderness, and streams in the wasteland." Through our difficult situations, right inside of them, His power and His change appear. He knows how to make us fulfilled, happy, content, and alive, but sometimes there's more ground to cover first. More distance to walk. More sand. In some cases, God's "new thing" springs up before we are even aware enough to notice it. That's why we have to keep stepping, keep jumping out in faith, keep placing our feet on the paths where His blessings are bound to sparkle if we simply open our eyes long enough.

I will keep stepping toward You in this night of uncertainty, Father. I will place my feet on Your path and pray that passion will soon be shimmering in drudgery's darkness. I will keep looking for Your "new thing." I will wait in faith, hoping the waters will return to this wasteland once again. But until they do, I will keep stepping. Stepping. Stepping. So many steps over ordinary sand, and then suddenly—somehow—one sparkles.

IN CASE YOU GET SIX MINUTES TO YOURSELF: STUDY GUIDE

1. Have you ever experienced a seemingly magical moment like the one described in this chapter?
2. Could you say that you are completely satisfied with your life right now? Why? Or why not?
3. Is it presumption to expect God to erase our difficult situations?
4. Read Isaiah 43:18, 19 in the greater context of chapter 43. What is God really saying to the people of Israel, and how does this apply to your life?
5. How do we find the patience to wait on the Lord when we are in the deserts and wastelands of life?
6. If God were to do a "new thing" for you today, what would you want it to be?

Flight

The little sparrow trapped in the airport terminal at gate A52 is perched on an east-facing window ledge, singing out to the rising sun. Below him on a cold plastic chair, I, too, am wondering just how I got so stuck and whether I'll ever find my wings once again. I would not call such a privileged journey as motherhood a trap. But nonetheless, through all the inexplicable joy and bottomless meaning and love, I have still somehow lost myself. It's just as easy to lose oneself in beauty as it is in hardship, I'd wager. And motherhood necessarily holds both, in balanced tension.

I am here without my children—which is an odd state to be anywhere these days. Heading home to them after four days away, heart expectant and arms already anticipating hugs. A three- or four-year-old boy beside me lines up his toy cars on the lowest window ledge, unaware of the tweeting bird above. I find myself alternately drawn to this boy and relieved that he is not mine, relieved that I am flying alone. I am free to thoughtfully browse terminal bookstores and able to think full thoughts without being interrupted—rare commodities. And yet I am lonely for my little ones, aching for those hands to tug on and wiggling bodies in seats beside me. Stuck between the free, childless woman I once was, longing for days of ease, and yet acutely aware of the need I have for my children. It's not that they complete me, because I do remember how to be me without them. It's more that they fill me up in ways that former pleasures cannot anymore. How many harried, hurried hours have I craved just a simple moment of peace? And yet, when I find one, or many strung together, I crave the very ones who disturb my peace.

Maybe motherhood has redefined peace for me altogether? It's not the absence of chaos and frenzy anymore, but rather the absence of worry or pain, the knowledge that my most-loved ones are nearby, healthy and safe and within arm's reach. I miss my freedom. I do. But I think I'd rather miss freedom forever than endure this awful longing for my babies.

The bird flits lightly from window to window, looking for a way out into the morning. I think of all I've willingly left behind to be with my babies: career and job opportunities, advances and recognition, paychecks and bikinis and sleeping in. What I miss most, I think, is that flying feeling of doing the things I was created for, the things I excel at, and the things that fill me with passion. My work once did that, and I feel it calling to me all the time, ever on the horizon, but there are still windows of time between us. I know those days will come back, when I choose them again. But I don't know whether I'll be the same person as I was when I left them. I can't say whether I'll be able to throw my heart into my work the way I once did, because my heart walks around now on eight human legs, carrying four tiny bodies to and fro. It's hard to imagine a day when my heart would be free enough to invest in anyone except them. And I'm afraid—afraid that when my chances do rise again, I'll be able to see them reflecting in time, but not quite soar into them. I guess I'm just afraid I won't know the way back.

The trapped bird lands on the top of a banner, causing it to sway gently above me, and my mind is on sheep—desert sheep—Moses leading them in Horeb's shadow away from danger, and ever away from his past. He was trained for leadership. As am I. He left leadership to herd sheep. I guess I've done the same. But when leadership found him again, when God's call came crackling through the fire, he didn't believe in himself anymore. He didn't want to go back; he was accustomed to the quiet family life in the desert of his own past. He didn't know how to lead anything but sheep (are people really so much different?), and he couldn't imagine mustering the strength it would take to overcome his fears. If God's call into full-time ministry came back to me again today, I suspect I would feel and react the same way: Not me, Lord—my lips will be too clumsy, my courage was lost long ago—send someone else.

As a teen on fire for Christ, I identified wholeheartedly with the call of Isaiah, not Moses. I read his story in the smoke-filled temple, and my heart exclaimed right along with him, "Here I am Lord! Send me!" But these days I definitely track more with reluctant Moses. I used to feel as though I really had a lot to give to the world, as he once did also, destined for greatness in Egypt. But now, when I'm giving all I've got to my kids, I don't know what's left, if anything, for anyone else out there. Most days end with me not only feeling empty but wondering how I'm ever going to be all my kids need me to be. The two responses vie for validity in my mind: "Send me!" "Send someone else."

Somewhere in the ever-clouding past of my own ministry training, I recall learning that Moses' objections to God's call came in five parts that day beside the bush. The first two objections were identity questions: "Who am I?" and "Who are You?" Oh, but those are still *such* good questions! Who am I, anyway, to be called by God, to go and do anything for God when I can lose my livin' mind over ten toy cars on the floor at bedtime? We ask that "Who am I?" question precisely because we already know the answer—we are unworthy, fundamentally flawed. We are not enough. Who am I to be responsible for four human beings? Who am I to deserve such joy? Who am I to raise these kids right? Who are any of us?

But the second question—"Who are You?"—is different. I think I know that answer, and yet, it is ever incomplete. I still continue to find more clues all the time, but there remains much mystery as well. Who is He, the One who calls us, the One who finds us in our ordinariness and self-doubt and somehow sees past it, sees right through it into the heart of us? Into the truest thing about us: that we were destined for a purpose of His design.

Moses' third objection is also a question—"What if they don't believe me?"—and a fair one at that. He's starting to think things through. Realizing all the flaws in God's plan (I've done this a time or two . . .). His fourth objection is merely a statement: "I am not eloquent," and he is right about that. It's too easy to state our shortcomings because we have to live with them all day. And they multiply. The fifth objection, the last, is simply a flat-out refusal: "Send someone else." Not me, Lord. Not me.

I can track with all of these objections, but it is some of God's responses that truly hit home for me. When Moses questions, "Who am I?" God quips, "I will be with you," as if to say, "Oh—it doesn't matter who you are. It matters who *I am*." When Moses queries, "Who are You?" God states plainly, "I am who I am." Another way to translate this is, "I will be whatever I will be." He doesn't give characteristics about Himself, as we would. He's more concerned about being and existence—being present, existing close, and yet remaining undefinable by human terms. His nearness is particularly important, because the nation of Israel is all but convinced that God has forgotten them. I, too, have toyed with this idea, left alone in an empty house with a toddler for too many days in a row. Did God only call me for a time that's passed? Did He forget me here? Is this one sheep all the flock He intended for me?

When I first left work unwillingly to stay at home with my babies, I resented one colleague who compared it to the quiet life of leading sheep. I didn't want to lead sheep; I wanted to do something important! Seven years later, I know this is exactly where I want to be—sitting on the floor in jammies midmorning with cuddly toddlers reading stories in my lap. This is *the* most important thing I'll ever do. While I miss the dawn of the workday, I absolutely want this more. I want this *most*. These days will not always be here, of course. At some point, I am going to have to find my way back out into the world again, instead of just looking on through the glass.

I'm looking through the toddler-sized window beside me now as my plane pulls away from the gate. The sun has risen over the Rockies, and the day arrived in pinks and periwinkles. I'm wondering whether the terminal bird will ever find his way back out into all this beauty. And then for some reason I can't explain, I am digging for my Bible stowed under the seat in front of me, and I am flipping to Isaiah 6, chasing something I haven't named yet. The words are not new. In fact, I have read this chapter so many times by now that I could probably quote most, if not all, of it exactly. But I'm reading it again anyway, because the Bible still stows surprises for me, hiding in the shadows of familiar stories, and I'm hoping one will jump out at me today.

It does.

Sometime just after takeoff—as the plane is climbing and I can see its shadow following on the ground beneath us and the Rockies stretching out in all their splendor at the edge of the sky—it hits me. The timing. The perfect, beautiful timing of God that is so simple to see in others' lives and so hard to see in our own. Isaiah has found himself in the throne room of God, with winged beings flying and singing praises all around, smoke billowing and doorposts shaking, and he is struck immediately by his own unworthiness. "Woe to me! . . . I am ruined! For I am a man of unclean lips, and I live among a people of unclean lips, and my eyes have seen the King" (verse 5). At this, a seraphim flies to Isaiah and touches his lips with a coal plucked directly off the fire and announces that Isaiah's sin is taken away. It is then, and *only* then, that God calls. And He calls in the form of a question, a survey of sorts. "Whom shall I send? And who will go for us?" To which Isaiah, cleansed and restored, now wholeheartedly volunteers, "Here am I. Send me!" (verse 8).

What strikes me so profoundly about this entire encounter is the fact that God did not call Isaiah until after He had met Isaiah's objections. He intended to call him all along—that's why He was there. He knew Isaiah's sin and was calling him in spite of it. But it was Isaiah who could not live with his uncleanness in God's presence; it was Isaiah who needed something to change before he could be freed to volunteer. And God understood that. He didn't even extend the call until Isaiah's objections had been answered. I've read this account more times than one could count, and I've never seen it this way.

So, God. You will meet me on the grounds of my objections. Perhaps You have all along intended to call me back anyway, but You know full well that I feel "ruined" and fearfully far from anything useful whatsoever. You know that I can't envision how motherhood and ministry could mesh together. You foresee just where my rusting talents and dried-up gifts will work again. And it doesn't matter to You that I feel unworthy, because you know that *everyone* you call is unworthy. And maybe it's best that we all know it well. But you still call us anyway. You meet us where we're faltering, touch our lips with new courage, and then You call us. This, of course, is exactly who I need You to be: the God who is familiar enough to find the faltering places in me and fortify them with Your immeasurable grace. The God who is capable of giving whatever reassurance I need before He calls me out into the world again.

The plane is soaring above the clouds, higher than any bird could ever fly, carrying me home to my babies and my life. And I am smiling from my window seat because I know that one day, someday, not terribly far from now, I will find my way back out once again.

And I will say Yes. Send me.

IN CASE YOU GET SIX MINUTES TO YOURSELF: STUDY GUIDE

1. What things have you left behind for motherhood? Do you miss these things, or were you glad to see them go?

2. What doubts do you have about yourself or your capabilities since becoming a mother? What would God say about these doubts?

3. Do you know what things God has made you for and called you to do? Are you doing them now, or expecting to do them later?

4. Read the calling of Moses in Exodus 3. Which of his objections do you identify with the most? Why?

5. Read the calling of Isaiah in Isaiah 6. If God's call came today, would you be able to exclaim "Send me!" or would something be standing in your way?

6. What might God be calling you to do today in your home and in your life, exactly as it is?